P9-DBO-491

PENGUIN BOOKS

BETWEEN WOMEN

Luise Eichenbaum, coauthor with Susie Orbach of *What Do Women Want: Exploding the Myth of Dependency* and *Understanding Women: A Feminist Psychoanalytic Approach;* and Susie Orbach, the author of *Fat Is a Feminist Issue* and *Hunger Strike: The Anorectic's Struggle as a Metaphor for Our Age,* are psychotherapists and the founders of the Women's Therapy Centre Institute in New York and the Women's Therapy Centre in London. They have lectured throughout the United States and Europe on women's psychology. Luise Eichenbaum lives in New York, and Susie Orbach in London. They have been best friends for more than sixteen years.

BETWEEN WOMEN

Love, Envy, and Competition
in Women's Friendships

Luise Eichenbaum
and
Susie Orbach

PENGUIN BOOKS

PENGUIN BOOKS
Published by the Penguin Group
Viking Penguin Inc., 40 West 23rd Street,
New York, New York 10010, U.S.A.
Penguin Books Ltd, 27 Wrights Lane,
London W8 5TZ, England
Penguin Books Australia Ltd, Ringwood,
Victoria, Australia
Penguin Books Canada Ltd, 2801 John Street,
Markham, Ontario, Canada L3R 1B4
Penguin Books (N.Z.) Ltd, 182–190 Wairau Road,
Auckland 10, New Zealand

Penguin Books Ltd, Registered Offices:
Harmondsworth, Middlesex, England
First published in Great Britain under the title *Bittersweet* by
Century Hutchinson Ltd. 1987
First published in the United States of America by
Viking Penguin Inc. 1988
Published in Penguin Books 1989

1 3 5 7 9 10 8 6 4 2

LIBRARY OF CONGRESS CATALOGING IN PUBLICATION DATA
Eichenbaum, Luise.
Between women: love, envy, and competition in women's friendships
/ Luise Eichenbaum and Susie Orbach.
p.   cm.
Bibliography: p.
Includes index.
ISBN 0 14 00.8980 2 (pbk.)
1. Women—United States—Psychology.   2. Friendship.
3. Interpersonal relations.   I. Orbach. Susie, 1946–
II. Title.
[HQ1206.E43   1989]
155.6'33—dc19   88–21845

Printed in the United States of America by
R. R. Donnelley & Sons, Harrisonburg, Virginia
Set in Janson

Dedication

This book is written in recognition of our relationship, our deep love for one another and in the hope that it will speak to other women.

Authors' Note

This book is an attempt to provide a feminist psychoanalytic understanding of the emotional and psychological processes that are set in train when women perceive differences in each other. It is about the difficulties women face in coming to terms with those differences. We hope it will enable women to handle those differences more productively and less destructively than is often the case at present.

It is *not* an account of differences between women. We have not attempted to discuss the particulars of class, race, and sexual orientation as they create divisions between women. Differences in background and in status are of course substantial and contribute to the hurt, the misunderstandings, and the anger frequently found in women's relationships today. The assumptions we make about one another often do not take account of these particular circumstances. The expectations, desires, and ambitions we have for ourselves are based on a perception of the world seen from the vantage point of an individual's class background, her economic situation, her sexual orientation, her race, the attitudes of her family, her age, her physical abilities and disabilities. We are often blind and ignorant vis-à-vis experiences dissimilar to our own; we may deny differences, we may misperceive the circumstances of others or, in our ignorance, we may collude with stereotypes. Certainly lesbians, working-class women, black women, and disabled women have suffered by being described thoughtlessly and stereotypically. Many women are often unwittingly written out of general accounts of women's psychology because of a failure to include them by referring either to the commonality of women's experience or to the particulars of their experience.

We hope that we are writing for all women, but we well understand that our conclusions reflect the scope and the limits of our clinical work in the United Kingdom and the United States. We write about the women we have met in the course of our work: women who come from a wide range of backgrounds, differing political persuasions and sexual orientations. We have worked with women mainly white, but some black, between the ages of twenty and sixty. Some have had no formal education past sixteen, others are first-generation, educated working class; many are newly professional women, and many are or have been housewives; some are unemployed, while others are involved in their own or their husbands' businesses. Family circumstances have varied just as widely. Some women, heterosexual and lesbian, live on their own, some live with their children, some live with their male or female partners' children, some are divorced. We have encountered these women in long-term psychotherapy, in short-term therapy, in couple therapy, in workshop settings, in conferences, and in work-based consultations.

We very much hope that women of all backgrounds, sexual orientations, and ages will find points of identification with the women we are writing about even if their own particular circumstances are not adequately described. We hope women will be able to read this as an *inclusive* account, and take what may be useful in our analysis into their own situation where specific differences in social and personal categories can be explored in more detail.

Acknowledgments

The authors would like to thank Gillian Slovo, Joseph Schwartz, and Caradoc King for their enthusiasm and labor at the beginning of the project, and Jeremy Pikser for his constructive comments, time, and energy in the last push.

Contents

BETWEEN WOMEN

Introduction

When we met sixteen years ago, when Luise was nineteen and Susie twenty-five, we had the air of free women about ourselves. We were full of the headiness of the early days of feminism and we involved ourselves in projects that would benefit women. We spent much of our time with other women learning and developing the new field of women's studies, discovering together a new way to see our personal histories and challenging our reflexive responses to almost everything. With a sense of risk and excitement, we gave our female friendships priority.

The world of the early 1970s in which we met turned our lives and our views of most things upside down. As a generation we put into practice ideas that had been beyond our imagination just a few years before. As students, our time was flexible. We spent whole days and nights with our friends, secure in the knowledge that our love affairs with men would coexist with our important female friendships, and that, if necessary, it was the men who would have to adjust and change in dramatic ways.

We remember the first times we saw each other at Richmond College[1] of the City University of New York. Susie was in a colloquium. A young woman, an undergraduate, read a paragraph she had prepared for an upcoming event to celebrate International Women's Day 1971. It was a powerful and passionate statement. Susie turned to her friend Carol Bloom, the Women's Studies coordinator. "That was good," she said. "Who is she?" "Oh, that's Luise Eichenbaum, she's in Women's Studies too."

And then, at a class on women in film, a young woman with a long suede skirt, tall purple boots, a trendy London shag haircut, an English accent, confidently commented on the film and what it had to say about women's lives. "Who *is* she?" Luise asked Carol. "That's Susie Orbach," replied Carol. "She's English and into politics and law and psychology." Luise was interested.

A friendship was about to begin that would affect us in profound ways for the next decade and a half of our lives. The special bond that formed in the earliest years of our friendship and the intensity of feeling between us still continues. The desire to chatter and share, to fill each other in on everything and seek each other's views is constant. Like women all over the world, we practice that particularly feminine skill of holding ten conversations and activities in our heads at the same time.

Our common work at the beginning of our friendship involved helping to build the Women's Studies Program. With our dearest friend Carol Bloom and the other women in the department we were engaged in creating the first baccalaureate degree in this new field. It was an energetic department that for a brief time expressed the very best energy of the Student and Women's Liberation Movements. Students became teachers, social barriers began to disintegrate, and women began to study and learn together in circumstances of their own creation. It was an exciting time. New educational policy was being made and we were doing the making.

But the program itself was headed for unanticipated difficulties. It had come into existence against strong opposition from the college administration. The reality of a successful program soon gave way to internal dissension and strife. The unity among the women that had been so essential to the successful launch of the program was soon shown to be ephemeral. It was a unity based on opposition to the administration rather than the expression of well-conceived and commonly held educational ideas. Political differences assumed tremendous significance and caucuses soon formed. Three factions disputed the direction of the program, crippling it. Meetings were rife with betrayal and anger. The women, all unused to wielding power within an institutional setting, seemed set upon destroying their common project.

We were shocked, devastated, and shaken. How could women, apparently with so much in common, be so destructive? How had our unity turned into a confrontation so very fast? What was the origin of the rage and disappointment that this dispute unleashed?

Perplexed and concerned, we were motivated to learn more about the psychological dynamics that occur between women. The more we understood about our social position, the more women's rational and conscious lives became comprehensible. Yet, we remained in the dark about women's unconscious lives and how they were entwined with those of other women. Our friendship and participation in the factional disputes of the program brought us closer together and strengthened our commitment to understanding both how the "outside got inside and the inside got outside."[2]

For the next several years we immersed ourselves in a new project—the study of women's psychology. Within this general project we particularly sought to understand the tension between women's strong and loving feelings for one another and the enmity that could suddenly occur. Together with other women who were feminists and psychotherapists,[3] we studied Freud's theories of psychoanalysis, although they were generally unpopular among feminists at the time; we studied humanistic psychology and alternative therapies, which were much in vogue; we went to graduate school and brought our interests about feminism and women's psychology into the classrooms. Throughout each area of study, a feminist perspective lead us to analyze, reevaluate, and reinterpret the theories of psychological development. With a perspective that included an understanding of women's social position, we began to develop a psychotherapy that could address the intricacies of women's complicated inner and outer lives.

Several years later in 1976, when we opened the Women's Therapy Centre in London, our intention was to provide psychotherapy that addressed the needs of women. To attract clients, we distributed flyers, we sent out press releases, we spoke on radio shows about why we saw the need for this kind of psychotherapeutic service. We were stunned by the response. The center attracted all sorts of women from different age groups and differing class backgrounds.[4] Some women who came had previously been in psychotherapy but had either had bad experiences or simply had not been helped. The center attracted women who were feminist and who now felt that they could undertake psychotherapy with a degree of trust and safety. Other women had no involvement in feminism but responded because they read an interview or heard us speak about an aspect of women's lives with which they could strongly identify. But even given the initial response, we had no idea of the enormity of the success the center would achieve. It is now in its twelfth year, receives both public and private funding, and is staffed by nearly a dozen psychotherapists and several administrators.

And our relationship grew. We were now united in a joint project which was stimulating, engaging, time-consuming. The popularity of the center found us involving two new psychotherapists, Sally Berry and Margaret Green, within just a few months of our opening, and later that year taking on two more, Margot Waddell, who was finishing up her training at the Tavistock Clinic, and the late Pam Smith, who came to us on leave of absence from the North London Polytechnic. Sheila Ernst was soon to join us as a trainee. We organized seminars for professionals on the psychology of women and workshops for the public. We were thriving. The problems began the following spring.

It seemed to begin out of the blue. We started feeling irritated with one another. Luise didn't like the way Susie could be curt on the telephone. Susie didn't like the way Luise hesitated over things. We began to look at one another critically, as lovers often do when the honeymoon is over. We began to snip at one another with increasing frequency and each night we went home to our men and complained to them about the irritating habits of the other. Partners, best friends. What was happening?

As it had in the Women's Studies Program at Richmond, the success of the project seemed to engender new, surprising problems. We spent three months of agony in the same small office, not knowing how to talk to each other. We did not know how to confront each other directly with the truth of our feelings. It was a torturous time. Finally, there was a reprieve; summer vacation was approaching and Luise decided to go back to the States for a visit.

In that month apart we complained about each other to friends, each frightened and unsure of what the outcome was going to be. But the distance also allowed other feelings to emerge. Missing. Loneliness. Pain. Hurt. Longing. When Luise walked through the door on a September morning, we looked at each other, paused, searched for a shared warm response. Then came the hug and the tears. Lots of tears. We declared our love, how we had missed each other, not only during the month, but throughout the four or five months. And then we talked. And then we yelled.

In the final analysis we saw that there was a common denominator to our anger. Each of us felt that the other was continually making assumptions. Luise thought that Susie assumed her agreement about things without asking her or checking to see if she really was in agreement. She seemed not to be aware sometimes that Luise had a different opinion. Susie felt that Luise assumed that Susie would take care of her in certain ways, taking the care giving for granted, as if Susie were her invisible magic mother, doing things for her without needing to be appreciated. We each felt lost inside the relationship, not visible. We were no longer individuated. In some powerful way our lives had been joined and even *merged*. We had not managed to remain separate individuals while birthing our new "baby," the Women's Therapy Centre. Our withdrawal and anger over a period of months was our attempt to separate ourselves, to distinguish us, one from the other. And yet if we had only retreated—as we were tempted to do—that would have meant the end of our relationship. Scared and anxious, we forced ourselves to struggle, to confront, to speak up directly to the other. We were lucky. Somewhere we were still aware of our need and love for each other. We knew we had to say, "Don't make assumptions, I am not you, I am not your mother, I am a separate person." We wondered why saying such things was so difficult. We did not know then what a critical lesson we had learned by acknowledging our individuality in our relationship.

Now it's 1988, eleven years after that first fight. There have been a few other occasions when we have each felt disregarded, misunderstood, or taken for granted. They are less frightening now and they build up over days rather than months. But they are still difficult to handle in the midst of the love and commitment we have toward each other. By now we've been best friends for more than fifteen years.

We've each lived and worked together in each other's countries. In 1981 with our old friend Carol Bloom we started up the Women's Therapy Centre Institute in

New York to train psychotherapists.[5] But although the two centers are a visible expression of the work we have done and do together, today we live an ocean apart. The three thousand miles between London and New York mean the loss of daily relating, of leisurely talking on the phone as often as needs be, of seeing each other at work, of preparing suppers together, of taking the kids to the zoo together, of traveling around either continent giving talks together, of shopping and chatting. The pleasure of being able to present our work to a new audience is tempered by the fact that we are doing so alone. Each paper written in our joint names evokes the pain of the separation. Each time Lukas (Susie's son) calls for Gina (Luise's daughter) or Gina for Lukas, tears are shed on one or the other side of the Atlantic. The children are little, but they have already grasped the importance of their mothers' friendship.

This book on women's relationships—the hope, the promise, the love, the grief, the anguish, and the disappointments, the reparative as well as the damaging aspects—had to start with a brief account of our relationship. For we write this book partly in celebration of the relationship we have enjoyed with each other and with our other women friends, of the pleasures that have come from working in female-centered environments and the wish to acknowledge the achievements of women at this particular moment in Western history.

This book is about the lives of women and their relationships with one another in the 1980s. It is about the legacy we carry from generations of women before us as emotional care givers, daughters, mothers, domestic laborers. It is about the rich ways in which women give to each other. It is about the ways in which women connect easily and intimately. It is about the pleasures women share together. It is about the virtues of femininity. It is, at the same time, about the lives of contemporary white, black, Asian, and Latin women in the Western world whose social roles have been dramatically changing in the last eighteen years. It is about the psychological reactions, conflicts, and struggles that women today inevitably confront in themselves. It is, above all, about the ways in which these social and psychological transformations are affecting women's relationships with one another. Contemporary women's friendships have been forged at a time when women's roles have been changing and women are demanding of themselves that they get out and fulfill themselves. It wasn't until the seventies that the significance of women's relationships was recognized. Of course women's friendships have always been important and essential, but until the seventies, friendship between women was rarely graced with the social recognition that befitted it. Friendships were fitted around family commitments and almost every woman understood that her time with a friend was limited.

The tremendous importance of women's relationships may not be prevalent in everyone's mind, so that many women continue to be isolated, but these relationships today are generally acknowledged and accepted. American films made in the 1970s, such as *Girlfriends*, *Alice Doesn't Live Here Anymore*, the French film *One Sings, the Other Doesn't*, the Norwegian film *Wives*, and televised themes in recent years ("Rhoda," "Kate & Allie," "Mary Tyler Moore" come to mind) reflect a cultural awareness of the significance of women's friendships. In these shows, women friends were seen confiding in one another, laughing with one another, and commiserating with one another. The friendships are not portrayed as a stopgap between sexual relationships but as an abiding part of a woman's life. Indeed, for many women, woman-to-woman relationships have become primary. Many women who a few years ago would have found it impossible to act on their sexual feelings toward one another now allow the erotic side of their feelings to emerge. Today, even though there is still considerable discrimination, lesbian relationships are becoming more visible and commonplace. For many women, closeness with a woman and the intimacy she finds in her friendships is deeply sustaining.

Paradoxically, while the media has presented female friendships with some accuracy, those very friendships are experiencing new difficulties that make them less ideal, less easy than they were a decade ago when there was something deeply liberating about sharing our difficulties and supporting one another. Today, enormous misunderstandings can exist between women. Part of our project has been to unravel, uncover, and speak openly about these difficulties. We need to address the sticky issues in women's relationships, the messy uncomfortable bits one wishes would just disappear; the hurt, the envy, the competition, the unexpressed anger, the feelings of betrayal, and the experience of abandonment. For along with the recognition of the importance of women's relationships in the last decade and a half has come the discovery that these relationships are not as easy and as trouble-free as we would wish. Behind the curtain of sisterhood lies a myriad of emotional tangles that can wreak havoc in women's relationships with each other. The hope we have invested in our relationships with one another, and the terrible upset we suffer when these relationships disappoint us must be understood in a context that respects and honors these relationships.

Connectedness, attachment, affiliation, selflessness have been and still are largely the foundations of women's experience. A woman knows herself and gathers a sense of well-being through her connection and attachment to others. For the past decade and a half or so, women en masse have been struggling to become more autonomous. Enormous amounts of time and energy have been and are currently being devoted to careers, education, advancement in areas that were previously the domain of men. Although the social environment appears more accepting of women's autonomy, the external prohibitions run deep. Women themselves embody these restrictions and constraints. And as women try to free themselves from the internal and external restraints, they find themselves acutely aware of the successes and achievements of other women. Women gauge and measure themselves in relation to friends, co-workers, neighbors. How does she manage a job, a relationship, and children? My best friend has a child— will I be able to? How much money does she earn? How does she manage to keep herself looking so well and fit when I feel exhausted? She seems so confident and self-assured while I feel like a fraud, a kid dressed up in grown-up clothes. These are the kinds of questions that women are asking daily. Many women are painfully aware of the emergence of negative feelings toward their women friends, feelings that serve to distance women, not bring them together, feelings that seem too ugly, too unacceptable to talk about.

To suddenly feel paralyzing guilt about a friend whose life seems to be going badly; to notice envious feelings exploding inside of oneself; to fear attack from those on whose support you rely; to feel competitive with a close friend; to experience terror that other women will abandon you or envy you—feelings such as these are formidable and are becoming commonplace. They are intensely experienced, and if they are not worked through, they are inevitably damaging. They erode and poison companionship. They threaten to destroy the openness and trust that can exist between women.

Women in the 1980s are making the shift from being people who service others, defer to others, and define themselves through their attachment to others, to becoming people who are visible in their own right and who stand as separate individuals while still connected to others. This is no easy feat. It is, however, what hundreds of thousands of women are engaged in doing, either deliberately or because of the impact of social forces on their lives. In this important struggle for change, we must not repudiate those who have most helped us get where we are today—women. But neither should we be squeamish about confronting the very real difficulties that can occur between women. Without sentimentalizing women's relationships, we can still declare women's continuing need for one another. Women need each other's support for the autonomy and self-development they are pursuing. They need each other to talk through the difficulties they are experiencing on so many fronts.

They need to explore the now-hidden feelings between women that threaten women's relationships. We can and must take on these issues, and in so doing preserve and nurture one of the relationships most important to us— that which is between women.

Chapter 1

Bittersweet

"Happy endings begin here," insisted Julie, a thirty-five-year-old drama teacher, toward the end of a Women's Therapy Centre workshop on difficulties in women's friendships. "They begin here in the confrontation of our negative feelings toward women we care about, not in fairy tale endings which suppress disagreement and pretend that everything is all right."

Although the center has a wide range of workshop topics covering numerous aspects of women's lives today, enrolling in a workshop on difficulties in women's friendships undoubtedly engendered feelings of anxiety and fear for the participants. Thirteen women gathered together to talk about the pain of jealousy, the pain of envy, the pain of anger, the pain of competition, the pain of abandonment, the pain of betrayal, and the pain of wanting when felt in relation to women. The upset in the room was palpable. Women were daring to face their negative feelings toward one another.

There were feelings of shame and disloyalty: "How

can I be discussing my best friend with a group of strangers." There was hesitation: "I don't know if I can put words to this feeling . . . I hate feeling this way, but I really am so hurt. . . ." There were feelings of bitterness and rage: "I am furious, how could she do that to me. . . ." There were feelings of being exploited: "How could she expect me to give and give and then not be there for me when I need her?" There were feelings of disappointment, of not being seen, of not being allowed to change, of sudden disapproval, of unaccountable and unexpected hurt. The workshop participants meeting for two consecutive Tuesday evenings were emotionally bruised, but as they engaged in the process of trying to understand what went wrong, why they hurt, whether friendship would always turn out this way, there was a relief stemming from the honest realization that women *do* have conflicting feelings for one another. The workshop was timely. A decade of open recognition of the importance and nurturing quality of women's friendships made it just safe enough to explore the underbelly of these relationships.

Julie described her amazement at seeing such a workshop on the Women's Therapy Centre schedule. It allowed shameful and impermissible feelings to be aired. But, she worried, would the whole world know she had negative feelings toward her dear friend if she enrolled for the workshop? Might she bump into someone on the way there, or worse still, at the workshop itself, thus exposing her conflicting feelings? Others felt the same, but reasoned that if the workshop was listed it must mean *other* women felt the same way; *other* women were in pain, angry, disappointed. Public recognition of these difficult feelings brought a great sense of relief.

Eleanor, a journalist in her thirties, wept as she talked of the fury she felt toward her friend Anne who had recently taken up with a new man. Everything she thought their friendship stood for was now swept aside as Anne broke dates and filled up their telephone conversations with gushing bulletins about the previous night's tryst. Really, it was too much, this going on about Jack. Christ, he wasn't even that interesting. "I know I'm probably jealous," said Eleanor, "but that's not the whole story. He's such a jerk. He isn't anywhere near good enough for her, and here she is head over heels and jettisoning our friendship or at least relegating it to the back burner. It feels like such a betrayal. It's not that I don't understand her infatuation and involvement or wish her well with it, I honestly do, it's just that I feel so pushed aside, not discarded exactly but like all of a sudden my function has changed. I'm there for her to replay it with, so she can savor the sex and excitement all over again. And even that I could understand, but I don't like that we don't do things together anymore, we don't go to the movies or plays, she and Jack do, we don't go out to a new restaurant, she and Jack do. I know I sound petty, but I do feel like our friendship didn't mean to her what it meant to me if she could just put it aside when he came along. It's like she was just using it as a stopgap not a pleasure in itself. I thought that was precisely what we weren't going to do."

"I feel let down and pushed out too," said Alison, "but I tend to see it as more my fault. Perhaps I was expecting too much from my friend Ruth. I have the feeling that I become so involved with my close friends that I almost push them away with the amount of need I bring to the relationship. Ruth and I used to see each other every day. We were in and out of each other's houses, borrowing children, milk, cars, lawn mowers, and sharing emotional traumas with each other. After we'd talked about it for months, Ruth went back to college and she really turned her back on me. At first I thought she was just so caught up in the newness of what she was doing and the work she now had to face, that I understood and tried to give her a bit of space. But then I had a crisis in my life, my mother was dying and I was very broken up about it. I told her—well she could see I wasn't coping too well—and she was kind, but cold. Instead of rallying, she just sort of told me to pull myself together. I was shocked and hurt. I felt so rejected. I felt like a big fat ugly mass of need, but I wasn't sure who was right or wrong. I'm still not, and that's why I'm here. I would have expected her to come through for me. Perhaps that's the nub of the problem. I have such high expectations of my friendships with women. I expect women to be giving and flexible. I felt I could understand her new need for some distance when she started college, but why couldn't she help me when my mother was dying? These high expectations I have of women really confuse me. Perhaps that's why I still feel so tortured after a year."

The internal dialogue gone over so many times as a way to understand the pain, to soothe the hurt, is voiced out loud now in this workshop setting with thirteen other women. There is something soothing in itself about having the other women eager to listen.

What happened in each of these friendships? How did they turn from supportive, nurturing mainstays to bitter disappointments? What is it that makes women's friendships what they are—both bitter and sweet?

Let's begin at the beginning. Two women meet, perhaps at a party, a class, over a backyard fence, or at a new
job. They share a mutual interest, and, with characteris-
tic feminine social agility, they extend their initial point
of interest to other matters. Their conversation takes
account of the emotional climate of the subject matter.
Thoughts and feelings about work, children, husbands,
boyfriends, lovers, about mothers, entertaining, cooking,
politics, sex, music, about aspirations, sports, fashion,
suffuse their conversation. Their emotions are intrinsic
to the contact. They make up a patois—a distinctively
women's language. Confidences are readily and easily
shared, assumptions made about difficult emotional
states, disappointments acknowledged, and solutions
sought. Women unguardedly confide in each other with
an ease that often astounds men. Sharing is not a conces-
sion, a particularly difficult struggle, an extraction;
rather it is part and parcel of women's relating. It is
second nature, a habit, a way of being. *Not* sharing feels
odd, a holding back that feels almost like a betrayal.

The texture of women's relationships, from the most
intimate friendships and love relationships to the most
cursory of acquaintances contain within them similar
elements, elements of compassion, sympathy, and identification. It is these elements, the emotional gullies in
which much female living occurs that allow us to talk of
a specifically female culture that has the capacity to em-
brace all women. In their journey through life, women
look for and find female companionship. From adoles-
cence onward young women have tried to understand
with one another the world around them. They seek a
bosom pal with whom they can giggle about the new
identities they are inventing and practicing. Closeness

with a peer becomes imperative. They seek their place in the world much as generations of young women have before them; they conceive of it within a network of relationships. As they take on school, dating, college, marriage, a first job, they do so with the enabling hand of a female friend. Perhaps a temporary friend soon to be forgotten, but whatever its longevity or circumstances, female companionship has more than likely been a distinctive feature of most women's lives.

Within their friendships, women talk uninhibitedly with each other about the details of sex, about what they want and what they have in their love relationships. They talk about their fears, their hopes for the future, their fantasies. Since early childhood women have learned to be attentive listeners and good givers and this is evident in their friendships where they can give each other support, understanding, comfort, sympathy, and advice. A woman gets a new job and she reaches for the telephone to tell her dearest friend; a woman discovers that her husband is having an affair and she reaches for the telephone to unload her distress on her friend; a woman wants to have an affair herself and reaches for the telephone to consult her friend about whether she should or shouldn't.

Women friends boost each other's confidence and help to smooth out the difficult emotional details of daily life. They discuss the inevitable problems and worries they have about their kids, they live through the pleasurable and obsessive details of planning and executing family functions. Women look after each other's children, help in the preparation of parties, go shopping together for food and clothes, discuss various aspects of their working lives. For many women, intimate relationships with women, friends, sisters, aunts, and co-workers are a bedrock of stability in their lives. The emotional texture of women's friendship is woven into the fabric of their daily lives. Indeed *a woman without a best friend is a very lonely woman.* There is an exquisite intimacy to female friendship, the sharing of experience, of daring, of pain, of challenge.

A deep friendship with a woman provides a sense of continuity. Unlike lovers and husbands, friendships may well survive the tumult of changing sexual partnerships that are so common today. But at the same time, friends are used to fading in and out of the forefront of relationships. Friendship offers a different kind of security than that of a sexual relationship. Friendship implies an unstated and unworried acceptance frequently missing in love affairs and marriage where the threat of the other leaving (or leaving oneself) often lurks. What distinguishes women's friendships is the easy reciprocity that envelops the relationship, allowing so many things to be safely discussed and felt.

Such is the positive, nurturing side of women's relationships. Women cooperate and support each other, and give each other enormous pleasure. But women's positive feelings toward each other have a counterpoint in equally powerful negative feelings. Women's relationships produce a rainbow of powerful emotions. The recent delight and recognition of the importance of women's relationships and the ideology of "sisterhood is powerful" has, in some ways, served to obscure much of the pain in women's friendships. But as much as we value and trust these relationships, we should be able to face the reality that they are not idyllic. They may provoke feelings of hurt and anger, envy and competition, guilt and sorrow. Women have been finding out at great cost that close friendships, work collaborations, and entire organizations can be disrupted, even destroyed by unexpected and unacknowledged negative feelings. When such painful feelings emerge in a work situation or friendship they can cause havoc and distress. The intensity with which they are experienced can be almost unbearable. And yet equally unbearable (or unthinkable) is the thought of talking directly to one's friend about the upset. For within women's relationships there seems to be more fear in talking about anger or hurt than there is within a marriage. And although many women may find it difficult to confront their sexual partners with critical or disturbing feelings on a regular basis, there usually comes a point when an explosive fight allows for the expression of them. Often within a couple relationship, women find an outlet for their anger or hurt through indirect means—by withdrawing sexually, for example. Or perhaps women can use crabbiness or a bad mood to indirectly communicate to their partners that something is not right. Yet rarely do we find ourselves acting similarly with a friend. We may withdraw by not telephoning as frequently, but when we do meet up, nine times out of ten we will have swallowed our upset, digested it in some all-too-familiar way, and will carry on without ever airing our feelings.

For several years women who had initially come together as students and legal workers to start a legal practice in Boston limped along, working together intimately on the barest of resources. As the practice prospered, and each week's payroll could be comfortably met, and projects could be pursued without the pressure of imminent financial collapse, differences grew between the lawyers and became both more obvious and less easy to tolerate. Just as at Richmond College, success itself seemed to breed unforeseen difficulties. In adversity the women could give each other unending support, discuss all the angles in a case and work late on preparing each other's briefs. It was in an apparently more relaxed environment that they saw the emergence of competition for the "interesting" cases, tussles over the use of the researcher's time. In short, various individual grievances eventually led to the dissolution of an attractive and nonhierarchical practice, leaving the eight members of the group feeling bitter and disappointed. It seemed as though women couldn't work together, and an experiment in sisterly principals had degenerated into petty disputes, time-keeping, and backbiting. Part of what made it impossible to keep the group practice together was the distaste and shock that accompanied the realization of the very strong negative feelings that arose. Warmth was replaced with suspicion, sisterliness with competition and envy, generosity of spirit with feelings of meanness and anger. But could it all have turned out differently? What could these women have done to save their organization and the important relationships within it?

Often women's feelings of anger, betrayal, envy, and competition toward one another occur most acutely in one-to-one relationships. Almost every woman can recall at least one occasion on which a friend told her of some good fortune and she was startled to discover that she felt uncomfortable.

A woman may feel she is going to scream, cry, or reach over and shake her friend when her friend tells her that she is pregnant. To be sure, Julie, the drama teacher, was delighted for her friend Wendy. That wasn't the point. For ages Wendy had wanted to have a baby. She'd actively searched for a partner with whom to start a family for three years. She had been trying to get pregnant for a year, since she had married Tom. But Julie was—inwardly—unaccountably envious. She didn't want Wendy to tell her that she was happy. She didn't want Wendy to bubble about midwives and doctors and baby's names. She didn't want Wendy to pull her into discussions about when she should stop working, how pregnancy was affecting her sex life, how tired she was, and how much she was eating. Julie wanted a baby herself. She wanted a man too and a job she liked and a new baby. She had a man she didn't like, a job she didn't like, and a teenage daughter who was a source of grief. She felt she'd had a baby far too young and now, with the benefit of mature insight and understanding, she ached to be in a situation where she could have a baby. All around her, her friends were having babies and to them life was exciting. She envied their energy and their enthusiasm. They all seemed capable of taking on so much and getting what they wanted.

Soon the pain of envy would be so difficult for her to bear that she would find herself not returning Wendy's calls and seeing her less frequently. Was the slipping away of this friendship unavoidable? What could Julie have done with her feelings of envy?

The way many women respond is to try to hide these feelings. Joanna, a potter, bore the pain of her envy privately. Her best friend Jenny, who'd been living with her lover Mary for five years, had finally successfully conceived through artificial insemination. Now it seemed, Jenny had everything going for her—a nice home, an interesting job in the media, a relationship, and a baby on the way. Joanna felt stuck in her work, couldn't seem to find a partner and was approaching forty feeling that she had not had a chance to decide whether or not to be a mother. When Jenny announced her pregnancy, Joanna showed no hint of envy. She was solicitous and kind during the pregnancy, knitted a few special jackets for the baby, and helped out with babysitting. But inside she was deeply jealous. Although she longed to have a baby, she didn't feel she should burden Jenny with her frustration. The most she could do was share her upset about everyone else having babies. On the outside she bore her envy of Jenny with dignity. On the inside she was in agony. But surely bottling up these distressing feelings can't be the only way to preserve a friendship.

The upset and envy that Julie and Joanna felt are not isolated instances. Increasingly, we encounter the angst of women in their late thirties and early forties who are facing a reality they did not foresee. A generation of women have directed themselves toward self-development in areas outside the traditional role of wife and mother, and although their working lives may be fulfilling, they can no longer postpone the decision of whether or not to have children. For some, life circumstances combined with age have made the decision for them. In many women there is a deep desire for children but they are without partners; for other women who perhaps are in couple relationships the desire itself is more conflictual. They feel ambivalent and find themselves weighing the pros and cons of having a child, the gains and the losses. This ambivalence can be paralyzing and yet they are terrified by the biological clock which refuses to stand still.

The childbearing years now commonly extend to the late thirties and forties. As a result, the decision of whether or not to have children is not being made simultaneously by this generation of women, which means that women are continually confronted by friends, colleagues, relatives who are pregnant and having children. An epidemic of powerful and deeply distressing feelings today surround pregnancy and childbearing in women's relationships. This is not to say that motherhood is the only source of envious feelings among women.

Envious feeling can be fueled by other major issues such as whether or not one is in a sexual relationship or whether or not one has a satisfying and well-paying job. Moreover, these feelings can erupt for what may appear to be much less significant reasons.

Friendship in adversity, unity in the face of opposition have been hallmarks of the positive side of women's relationships. The difficulties that can occur when women or women's groups do well (and not badly), or the upset that is unleashed when differences surface in a relationship that was built on shared suffering, are realities women are now beginning to grapple with in an attempt to understand themselves better and preserve valuable relationships. But it is a reality that is often easier to ignore than to confront.

To understand how this has happened, we need to consider the impact of changes in women's social role on their relationships with each other. Alongside the gains of self-development, new areas of difficulties, new conflicts, and new sorrows are emerging. We need to provide ourselves with a social and psychological perspective that can account for these changes. And we need to go further, we need to see the ways in which women are grappling with these new realities, the difficulties that are now arising in one-to-one relationships, in women-run work settings, and in business and professional contexts. Women have become accustomed to relying on each other for the fulfilling of many different needs. Women have enjoyed the intimacy that exists in their relationships. The strengths in those relationships combined with an accurate analysis of the current situation will allow us to confront the difficulties so that we can resolve them and move these crucial relationships forward.

Chapter 2

New Expectations

Whether or not one felt oneself to be a part of the Women's Liberation Movement, few in Western society today remain untouched by its ideas and demands. We have all witnessed one of the most radical decades of change for women this century. In many ways, ideas that at one time seemed drastically revolutionary have been incorporated into the very fabric of our homes, work places, schools, and art. Images of the bra burning, man-hating feminist have faded and in their place we see a woman with a briefcase in hand, putting in a hard day's work at the office, an exercise workout scheduled into her busy day and coming home to a liberated dishwashing husband and the kids; or a woman with a hard hat and work boots skilled in a trade that is new terrain for her gender. It is unclear and indeed perhaps irrelevant to ask whether these women consider themselves feminists. They are just modern women living the lives they have come to expect for themselves and which are expected of them.

Indeed, women today are faced with a barrage of contradictory images of femininity. Women are executives; women are mothers; women are independent; women are weak and dependent; women are secretaries; women are engineers; women are sexually confident and liberated; women are loose and whorelike; women wear spiked high heels; women wear men's style shoes; women wear silk teddies and lacy stockings; women wear tailored suits; women use their own American Express® cards; women are doing the laundry and chauffeuring the kids; women pay housekeepers to do that work for them; women are other women's housekeepers. The list is endless but its meaning is clear. Women today are living in the heart of a social tornado. We've uprooted the old definitions which imprisoned us and we are struggling to find our new and rightful place in the world outside as well as inside the family. We are straddling two worlds.

Newspapers and magazines announce that the women's movement is over, that the struggle for equality is won.[6] But women have learned that achieving status in the work place and at the same time remaining committed wives and loving mothers is often unbearably demanding. And the media, ever-hungry for new markets and new stereotypes, have compounded the pressure by surrounding us all with images of the new Superwoman, who not only has a loving husband, a spotless home, and cared-for children, but also a high-paying, high-powered career. The enormous stress of these new expectations is becoming obvious as the incidence of heart attacks and lung cancer goes up for women.

But where are we to get the strength to be today's Superwomen? Those of us who were involved at the beginning of the women's movement gathered strength from *sharing* our common experiences. It broke down emotional isolation, and we found courage in our connection with each other. Where there was only one woman there were feelings of inadequacy, self-hate, passivity, fear. When she connected with others in a group there was revelation, understanding, empathy, rage, pain, unity, and a new sense of power. We began to look at other women differently, as people we could value, and in so doing we began to value ourselves. We were being transformed on an individual and social level.

Are women today still getting that same strength from each other's support? Perhaps the greatest conflict women are facing now as a result of the movement's explosive impact is the crisis in their relationships with one another. As we have seen in chapter 1, women are capable of achieving intimate relationships and deep friendships with one another. Recently, books have appeared which tell us of the need to honor friendships and to recognize that men have something to learn from women in this area. Feminist theoreticians have pointed to women's capacity to connect, to give, to relate intimately, and the need for our society to value these feminine qualities. Women's role as nurturer and mother has always provided women with the skills and opportunities to relate and not fear emotional connection. Long before the women's movement, women achieved deep and significant friendships. Mothers and daughters, sisters and aunts, friends and neighbors relied on one another for practical and emotional support. Then, through the women's movement, women's connections deepened still further. As women revealed their most private thoughts and experiences they broke through to new levels of intimacy. Nothing had to be hidden. Women talked about the most intimate details of their sexual lives and fantasies, they exposed what went on behind the scenes in their marriages and relationships with men and other women. No area was verboten.

But something has changed. In our practice we hear women talk about new issues that they dare not discuss with their closest women friends. There is a post-feminist self-imposed censorship on certain feelings that women consider unacceptable. Feelings, for example, of competition and envy are rampant. No woman today escapes them, but every woman feels conflicted by them. Feelings such as these cause tremendous pain and confusion for all women today. There is a new privatization of women's experience, but this isolation is not identical to the old isolation. It is similar in that just as before women are experiencing self-doubt, self-blame, feelings of inadequacy, envy of other women. But this time around the conflicts are more complex. There are stronger forces at odds.

During the height of the women's movement as we moved from a position of isolation to one of comradery with other women, our sense of entitlement grew. We knew that we were fighting to open doors that had been closed to our mothers. Although many of them had worked—either from economic or personal need—only rarely and individually had women been employed in areas reserved for men. When we walked through those newly opened doors we did so with great trepidation, but in contrast to them we also had a sense of a movement behind us. The movement was our security blanket—we could have it with us as we took new and scary steps out into the world.

This world had been occupied by men for centuries. Our realm was supposed to be the home while theirs was the marketplace, and now here we were in foreign territory. Women had been here before but in far fewer numbers and in a different way. They had been the exceptions and had been regarded as unwomanly. As a movement we proudly and loudly announced ourselves *as women* before our arrival, and we were met with an array of responses. We were teased when we insisted upon being called women instead of girls, but we persisted and we were called women. We gritted our teeth as male colleagues and bosses purposefully or unconsciously undermined our efforts and confidence as they examined our work with fine-toothed combs, ready to jump on us for the tiniest of mistakes. Other male colleagues, aware of the powerful movement from which we'd come, recognized the contribution to be made and revealed their more progressive discomfort by relating to women with a kind of awe or reverence.

Nevertheless, although on one level we had a movement behind us, on a day-to-day level we were in those jobs on our own. Each woman had to meet the challenge of her particular circumstance and in order to survive she had to find her way in the foreign land of the masculine work world. She had to learn the ropes—working doubly hard to prove her competence. She had to adapt to the rules of the game in order to get in and stay in. She was entering a world that had a history and a very particular ethos of competition, an ethos often at odds with the ethos of what it has previously meant to be a woman. It is a world with clearly demarcated rules of deference and rank where one does not dare expose vulnerability or compassion for fear of losing one's place on the ladder to promotion. In this new, unemotional world, the bonds between women are broken. In the world of every-woman-for-herself, the old support systems can be tragically undermined.

Ann Russell, a senior vice-president with a mainstream publishing house, is a very successful woman. A robust, warm, and extremely convivial woman of fifty-seven, she began her career as an editor when her second child started kindergarten. She soon became a senior editor, and four years later was promoted to editor-in-chief. Throughout each of those promotions she was friends with a group of women colleagues. When Ann became editor-in-chief, there was a noticeable shift in her relationship with her friends. Both she and her friends kept up with lunch dates but they were less frequent. When Ann was promoted to senior vice-president, the change was even more noticeable. For the first month or so she was too busy adjusting to her new work responsibilities to arrange a date with her friends in editorial. As the weeks went by, the distance increased. One day she was out to lunch with an author when she noticed all three of her old friends at another table, sharing stories about their day, their home lives, their latest shopping trip, or a new book or film. Her heart sank and she felt utterly desolate. She was outside, no longer a part of the group. The mere fact of her success had cut her off from her women friends. Ann lived with a loneliness she had never before experienced at work.

Ann's success story is not uncommon these days. In our practice, we are increasingly hearing about the problems women are experiencing in their relationships with other women as they become more successful in their careers. Clearly, Ann was paying a high price for her success. But why? Is this price inevitable?

Over the past decade, more and more women have achieved a status that previously had been for men only. Competence in the work place is not an image women have deeply imprinted in their sense of what it means to be a woman. In the past, images of successful women have been more usually linked with glamor than professional competence. Forceful women at center stage have often been defeminized, making it hard for the ordinary woman on the job to identify with her. It cannot have escaped our attention that the three women leaders of the 1970s and 1980s, Golda Meir, Margaret Thatcher, and Indira Gandhi were all involved in wars—the ultimate masculine activity. Thus, women in the public eye are often a long way from the role models ordinary women might wish to emulate. But now that women anticipate being in the work force for many more years and work is a source of crucial aspects of their identity, they are increasingly confronted with female superiors who they may wish to emulate or surpass. There are, for the first time, significant numbers of female bosses. This is a new kind of relationship for women, and it is not always easy to negotiate. Women superiors take on the mantle of role model whether or not they envision themselves this way. And for those on the way up, the feelings of competition and envy, the scurry for approval, the wish to be acknowledged and noticed by other women are now a part of their daily work lives. These emotions can be troubling and confusing, and often lead to real problems on the job, which in turn affect women's new sense of self.

Elaine was an editor at Ann's publishing house. She

had a list of lucrative authors and was accustomed to dealing with contracts involving large amounts of money. She herself had brought in two best sellers that made her company a great deal of money. Her own salary did not reflect the kind of contribution she made and yet she was extremely nervous about asking for a raise. She alternated between feeling grateful that she had a good position and feeling furious that her contribution was not being financially rewarded. In addition, she was angry at herself, realizing that a man in her position would hardly be acting this way. Although she didn't understand it at first, central to her passivity was the effect on her of having to ask a woman executive officer— Ann—for a raise. She felt Ann should recognize her contribution to the company and reward her without prompting. She felt Ann should know how she felt. Somehow, she almost felt, that if she had to *tell* Ann she deserved a raise, maybe she didn't really deserve it after all.

It took Elaine months to pluck up the courage to discuss a raise with Ann, at which point she did it in a mealy-mouthed way, trembling inside. She got the raise. Six months later there was an office reorganization and a man was now responsible for salary decisions. Elaine had brought in yet another best seller and she believed that she had been too timid in asking for her last raise. She found herself one day in her new boss's office asking for an increase without having even prepared herself for it. She was surprised by her own forthrightness. As she left the room, raise negotiated, she reflected on how differently she had acted in this situation compared with six months earlier. She could hardly attribute the change to confidence arising out of the previous encounter nor to any particular kindness on this man's part. The only thing that could account for the difference was that he was a man and her previous negotiation had been with a woman. What this meant and why she felt insecure in front of a woman and confident in front of a man perplexed her. It was the exact opposite of what she imagined would be the case. It was as if displaying her confidence to another woman was dangerous, somehow forbidden.

Women in positions of power can be placed on a pedestal as a result of the admiration of other women. Once there, the woman principal, the professor, the account executive, the head buyer, the senior administrator, the chemist, and so on, becomes the object of a range of feelings from those other women. Sometimes a female superior is seen as an enabling and inspiring figure in that she has shown that a woman can succeed. But just as often the inspirational aspect gives way to feelings of jealousy, of anger, of wanting what that woman has. The woman becomes the focus of enormous amounts of interest and gossip. Her private life and her work actions assume importance out of proportion with reality. She becomes a figure of fascination and interest to those around her. A woman placed in such a position can become extremely isolated. Other women cease responding to her as one woman to another, instead she has to relate through a quagmire of projections and fantasies. When she casually shares some vulnerability with a colleague, the colleague may be stunned, not imagining that her boss could possibly feel that way. It is as if being in a position of authority and power at work, she is no longer a woman.

But even in women-run businesses, which have a less

clearly masculine orientation and less masculine work styles, we are now coming across situations with similar psychological themes. These new work-related problems have to be tackled if women's enterprises are to continue to be successful.

Rena, a black New Yorker, was employed as a personal assistant to the boss of a small interior design firm. She was a year or so older than her boss, had less formal education, but was full of energy and spunk. The job gave her plenty of opportunity to move from administration into planning or marketing. She'd been attracted to the job because it had the potential to be what she made it. Her boss Margie chose her because she seemed talented and able, had a good sense of humor, and apparently had plenty of initiative. But when she actually started working, Rena was less happy with the job than might have been expected. As she put it, she underperformed and did not really take advantage of the opportunities the job held for her. Margie felt the same way and regretted that Rena contributed less than they might both have wished. On the job, they had a companionable relationship, but why couldn't the wonderful collaboration they'd both wanted come to be?

In her therapy Rena talked about how incompetent she felt around Margie and how she felt she was always finessing her shortcomings, and expecting to be found out. She admired Margie greatly and had really aspired to be like her. When she first came to work for her she dreamed of making a good enough contribution that they could become partners. She was impressed with Margie's confidence, which she believed was real and solid, as opposed to her own, which felt very superficial and shaky. She wanted what Margie had and part of what had attracted her to this job was the hope that Margie could give it to her.

In reality, Margie's confidence was almost as fragile as Rena's. Although her company was successful, she was quite scared by its expansion. Part of her reason for offering Rena such an open job description was fudging; she was herself uncertain which direction Rena should go. She was unwilling to give the kind of leadership that would allow herself, Rena, and the company to grow. Although she projected the knowledge and competence provided by her private education, she was the first woman in her family to seriously work for money. She enjoyed both the actual design work and the contact with clients, but she couldn't conceive of herself as an employer who was building an expanding company.

Rena needed direction from Margie and was disappointed and confused when she did not receive it. She continued to hold Margie in awe and to see her as perfect. She liked Margie's easygoing attitude, and she envied the ease with which Margie ran her business. But to Margie herself this attitude betrayed a lack of ambition. She saw it as an expression of timidity, a failure to take advantage of the business opportunity she had created, and she felt guilty toward Rena, whom she felt she was failing. Both women had expectations of Margie that Margie was unable to meet. Rena reacted by blaming herself and putting Margie on a pedestal. Margie also blamed herself. Their need to hide their insecurities from each other undermined the authenticity of their relationship and sabotaged the success of their collaboration.

Women's greater involvement in the work place has affected their relationships outside it as well. Women

find themselves engulfed by work commitments, preoc-
cupied with issues related to work and the driving energy that propels them to be more ambitious. Women
who have partners or children find that work and family
commitments leave less time and energy for their friendships with other women. Relationships, which at one
time seemed so central to daily life, drift away, held
together by a thin thread or ended. Even the memory of
how these relationships made us feel, how they fed us
emotionally and allowed us to feel our own person, separate from our mates, can fade.

Eva comes home from her job at the telephone company at six o'clock, greets her two young children and
husband, and sits down to hear the chaotic report of each
person's day. Her husband, Tom, quickly mentions that
she got a phone call from her best friend Andrea and
goes on to tell her about a talk he had with his boss. Her
daughter shows her a book report she wrote at school
that day, while at the same time her son tries to tell her
about his dentist's appointment. She wonders if she'll
manage to call Andrea back and hates the feeling that a
phone call to her dearest friend is yet another pressure.
She's exhausted from a long day's work, but makes a
great effort to be attentive to her family. She knows that
the children are extremely demanding because they
haven't been with her all day and they want and need a lot
from her. She uses all of her self-control just to keep from
screaming at everyone to shut up. All she needs is a little
peace and quiet, a few moments to relax and unwind.
She knows she can't have that. She and her husband get
dinner together, they all sit down to eat. After dinner
her husband cleans up while Eva bathes and prepares the

children for bed. By 9:00 P.M. the kids are asleep and Eva collapses onto the sofa. She thinks about Andrea, her dearest friend of twelve years. Earlier in the day she had thought about how she wanted to make a date to see her, something they try to do regularly—only "regularly" has changed over the years. It used to be at least once a week with a phone call every day; now for each of them, with work and family, it's an effort to meet once a month. Eva summons all the energy she's got left and goes to the phone. They speak for a few minutes, commiserating about their exhaustion, fill each other in on a few recent developments, and say they must make a date. They each get their diaries and turn from one weekly page to the next in an effort to come up with an evening that's good for both of them. Between work-related appointments, meetings, and family commitments, the date must wait nearly three weeks. With frustrated resignation they say goodbye and promise to speak again in a couple of days.

Everyone in her own way has had to adjust to the new demands of the modern woman's life. One of the results of the success of the Women's Liberation Movement has been the ability of women to choose more freely when, how, and if they have families. But on the other hand, this freedom has lead to a diversity that is not always easy to bridge. We saw in chapter 1 how painful it was for Julie to listen to the news of Wendy's pregnancy. In our practice we increasingly hear women talk about their loneliness and their reluctance to intrude on a friend's life, particularly if one woman is single and the other is involved with a family. Single women with children have the additional stress of single-parenting and many of their coupled friends are often unavailable to them. Whereas the coupled woman may emotionally depend upon both her partner and friends, the single woman may have only her friends to rely on for relational intimacy. The women she depended on so strongly a decade ago seem immersed in pregnancies, kids, partners, and work.

Single and divorced women may feel the lack of female friendship much more acutely than women in families. Alison is thirty-three. She recently separated from her husband and has been painfully adjusting to the breakup and to living alone. Her two closest friends are married. The women had been a threesome from their early twenties and had been through many ups and downs together. New men came and went but the "girls" were always there. As each married, their relationships to one another adjusted to their new lives. The women brought the men into the group and the couples spent a lot of time together. Since Alison and Jack split up, she's seen them all a lot less frequently. Many nights when Alison returns from work she experiences anxiety upon entering her apartment. Some nights it's more severe then others, but each time Alison desperately feels the need to phone someone, to make contact, to feel less alone. For the first couple of months after Jack moved out, Alison felt it was all right to phone one of her two friends. They understood what a difficult time she was going through. But after several months Alison began to feel that she could no longer call them so freely. She knew that they were each tired from a day's work and needed to relax with their husbands. She could hear the exhaustion in their voices and sensed that they didn't have enough energy left to take care of her. She imagined that they were beginning to feel annoyed with her. She sat alone in her pain and upset.

Concrete differences like work and families are not the only obstacles between women. The new expectations of today's women, the fantasies and projections of themselves and others, can form a barrier to friendship.

Marilyn and Arlene work in the same occupational therapy unit. Each has had considerable emotional difficulty meeting the demands of her job. Each of them yearned for a good friend to confide in, but their images of each other got in the way.

Marilyn is forty-eight, married for twenty-six years, and the mother of three grown children. She returned to school to get a postgraduate degree in occupational therapy when her youngest child was in high school. When she got her first job she was thrilled beyond belief. After twenty years of being at home raising children and three long hard years at school she was finally entering the work force in her own right. Her husband and youngest son, who still lived at home, had to adjust their schedules to hers. They all had to discuss who was going to shop for dinner and who would be home earliest to prepare it. The picture had changed dramatically. No longer was everyone else in the family out while Marilyn maintained the home front. Now she, like them, had another dimension to her life.

When she got her first paycheck she felt like she had just won the Nobel prize. She discussed with her husband how each of their salaries should be used, knowing that she wanted to maintain a substantial portion of her salary for personal use. Earning a wage and having a job outside the home seemed to have a snowball effect on Marilyn's life. She found that she was in a position to make decisions about various things on her own whereas previously she would have felt obliged to check with Abe first.

For Marilyn, the move from being a housewife to having a job outside the home gave her a profoundly new sense of herself as a person. She rediscovered facets of her personality that had laid dormant for decades. Marilyn enjoyed a vitality and energy that she hadn't felt in years.

But the process of internal change, change of one's psychology, one's sense of self, is often excruciatingly slow. It goes without saying that Marilyn's new connection to her job had a forceful impact on her. But Marilyn was coping with change on two sides—her role in her home and her relations with her family; and her new responsibilities at work. She had to grapple with feelings of guilt toward her son and husband for not being constantly available and for her tiredness at night. She would find herself doing the laundry at ten o'clock at night, or running frantically to shop for food during her lunch hour. Somewhere inside she knew that these things were not essential and yet she could not stop herself from doing them. At work she struggled with her lack of confidence as she gazed at colleagues in disbelief when they sought her opinion about a course of treatment. It took a long time for her to overcome feeling that she was playing some kind of game which would shortly come to an end. After she agreed to deliver a paper at a conference of occupational therapists, she couldn't sleep for a month. She was so anxious that she couldn't think of anything but the presentation and had nightmares about losing her voice or fainting on the platform. She looked at her younger colleagues, such as Arlene, and imagined that they felt infinitely more self-confident than women of her generation. She envied the ease with which these young women moved around in a world that used to be for men only. She couldn't imagine that they suffered the anxieties that women of her generation experience. Younger women seemed to have an air of self-assuredness and entitlement. They were ambitious and didn't feel they had to even think about having children until they were thirty.

Meanwhile, Arlene had her own feelings of insecurity and her own fantasies about who Marilyn was and what she felt. Arlene went to graduate school directly after finishing her undergraduate studies. She had become interested in occupational therapy as a sophomore in college when her favorite aunt suffered a nervous breakdown and was helped by an occupational therapist during her hospitalization. Like Marilyn, Arlene came from a working-class family. Her father was a bus driver and her mother worked for Con Edison. She was the first in her family to go to college and into a white-collar profession. Although she knew that she did her job well, she was still riddled with the feeling that she was fraudulent in her relations with her co-workers. She would hear her own words echoing when she spoke to someone on a professional basis. It was almost impossible for her to believe that she was a highly trained and qualified person. She carried her mother in her head and could not help but feel that she was out of place in this world of sophisticated, middle-class people.

Arlene imagined that as an older woman Marilyn felt confident and was ripe from experience of the world. She respected her, as did other workers, both male and female, because she was older. Arlene's unarticulated assumption was that women of that generation had not had to struggle with the awful decision about whether or when to have children. Marilyn had had her children and now, Arlene assumed, she'd satisfied that part of herself and was free to concentrate on her career. She wasn't thirty and single and desperately watching the biological timeclock ticking away. She'd been married to the same husband for twenty-six years and didn't have to deal with the god-awful singles scene, looking for a man who doesn't exist.

Arlene and Marilyn, despite their different ages, share more than they know. These women are situated on different spokes of the same wheel—the wheel of women's changing social role. Each spoke contains its own pressures, both internal and external. There are differences and there are similarities. A woman's age, her class, and her race may place her on a different spoke in the revolution of the wheel to which she brings varying expectations, restrictions, desires, and dreams. The emphasis of change has been on what she can be. But who she is, how she feels about herself, how she manages the new possibilities in her life are greatly affected by the underlying sense of who she is as a woman in our society.

Over the past fifteen years, women have undergone changes that go beyond a superficial level (who wears a bra and who doesn't), beyond a social level (who does the dishes), and into profound changes on the psychological level, profound changes in the very meaning of gender. Gender is not simply a matter of sex roles. Sex roles are a set of functions and activities, which are determined by any given culture, for the males and females within that culture. As a gendered person, a girl or boy grows into a sex role. The challenge to and change in women's sex roles over the past decade has had an impact on women's internal sense of self. Girls and women continue to recognize themselves as feminine—that is, their gender has not become confused—but the *meaning* of femininity has changed. Femininity is a deeply profound sense of oneself as of the feminine gender, as female. Hand in hand and inseparable from the development of a sense of self, of I, of a personality, is one's sense of oneself as a gendered person. We come to know ourselves in the world as either feminine or masculine and gender is a primary structural building block within our personality, our psychology.

Obviously, femininity is not simply a matter of clothes or makeup. Historically, however, grooming and external appearance have been crucial indicators of how women have felt about themselves as women. How women's attitudes to these external trappings of femininity have changed over the last fifteen years serves as an interesting paradigm for the changes in the meaning of femininity itself.

At the beginning of the Women's Liberation Movement, we rejected out of hand everything that we understood as society's definition of feminine. Although we may have called ourselves feminists, we sometimes seemed to accept the notion that feminine had to mean weak, passive, unserious, and artificial. We wore masculine jeans and work boots and went natural, wearing no makeup, and no longer shaving our legs or our underarms; we took off our bras. It was as if we had to throw off the old dress to aid us in throwing off the old ways of being. We clung to the new code of women just as our mothers clung to the old code.

Having this new code, this new uniform was important to us. It helped us to feel that we were a part of the women's movement; being accepted by other women provided a sense of security that each woman yearned for. The movement itself symbolized a good mother who could be proud of her femininity, her womanliness, her strengths; a good mother who could encourage us to stretch ourselves and to develop in areas in which we had previously felt so prohibited and undermined; a good mother with whom we could identify and feel connected; a good mother who held out her arms to hold us and have us be a part of a loving, positive, securely feminine, woman's world. Sisterly appreciation and love for other women was food for our own efforts toward self-love.

The self-acceptance gained through our relationships with one another allowed deeper feelings of self-confidence and those feelings, in turn, led to steps of autonomy. Women began to develop inner feelings of solidity, feelings that could only have come from that first step of love and acceptance by other women. As each woman internalized the attachment to other women in a secure way she was able to feel more of her own person. From this more secure base, she could risk steps toward further self-actualization even if these steps took her out of the cocoon of women's (the new mother's) arms. Just as an infant having first known itself through mother's reflection moves on to develop a unique and differentiated self, so too did women, full of other women's positive reflection and love, move on toward steps of differentiation.

Revealingly, as women started to differentiate, they started to let go of the rigid external uniform of early feminism. Surely, there were pangs of guilt as women shaved their legs or put on eye makeup. Did this mean we were backtracking? Did this mean that the movement was over and we were merely returning to the old ways of femininity? Not really. We were following an impulse, a desire that both helped us to individuate within the movement while it reconnected us with aspects of our mothers whose lives we felt we had so profoundly rejected. In some ways, our rejection of our mothers and their lives was being turned around as our anger toward them changed to an understanding of their limits, of their lives as women just like us. We were unconsciously attempting a synthesis. After a decade of criticizing the damaging and oppressive effects of the old femininity, of rejecting it and attempting new definitions, we needed to consolidate. We needed to chew over and digest all that we had taken in. Consciously, we knew that we had come a long way and that it was possible to be a strong, self-loving, competent woman who also shaved her legs or wore makeup. These traditional feminine characteristics did not have to be the sole determinants of who we were to be as women as they had been in the days before the movement. Reclaiming the feminine as a part of us was another step in the evolution of women's sense of self. We no longer had to reject one code of femininity and adopt, en masse, an opposite code in order to be able to feel the strengths, the entitlement, the self-assuredness that we wanted to feel. Differentiating from other women, from friends, was a developmental step. By gaining the love of other women, we could love ourselves. By gaining the nurturance and permission from other women to move ahead, we were able to grow. We could allow ourselves to embody the femininity of our mothers and generations of women before them as we embodied the new images of womanhood we were creating.

Although women's lives are still largely constrained (and this is more or less true depending on one's class or racial background), women today are freer to make more choices in their lives now than perhaps at any time in history; choices about career, sex roles, sexuality, motherhood; choices about what it means to be a woman. The change from a social role in which the mandate was connection to others, availability to others, self-deference and support for others, to a role that includes self-actualization, self-interest, entitlement, and desire for a place in the world as well as in the family, requires differentiation. And differentiation defies the very essence of feminine psychology. Prohibitions against women's autonomy and position in the world outside of the home as separate, effective, substantive people are dynamic forces in this new complication in women's relationships. Do we have to pay the price of having one or the other? That is, can we be people in the world without engendering envious, competitive, and resentful feelings in our women friends? Do we have to lose the very people from whom we desperately need continued support? Have the recent changes in women's social position produced irreparable gaps in women's relationships with one another? We think not. But in order to bridge those gaps, we need a deeper understanding of the psychological meanings of women's attachments to each other.

Chapter 3

Merged Attachments

How can we understand two phenomena: the easy, comfortable, and cozy feelings that women can create together and the difficult misunderstandings that can shatter those feelings? How is it that women can feel the preciousness and importance of each other's support one moment and feel anger, envy, and betrayal at another? What motivates women's desperate need for each other and their disbelief that they can have the acceptance they so want from one another? How can we understand the closeness between best friends and the bitter repudiation of that relationship in a falling out?

Women's positive feelings for each other undoubtedly outweigh the difficulties that they are now encountering with one another, but it is important to understand that the latter are not an aberration of the former or a negation of them. The truth is that these feelings share the same roots. The developmental and social processes that are at the heart of women's easy connections are the *very same processes* that are at the heart of their difficulties with one another.

An Ordinary Encounter

Sheila, a thirty-year-old illustrator, is lunching with her friend Rose who is also thirty, married, and works in advertising. Most of the conversation centers on Rose's frustration over not getting pregnant: she's been trying for six months. As they are getting ready to leave the restaurant a woman with two small children walks in and sits down at the next table. Rose and Sheila smile at her in acknowledgment both of the cuteness of the kids and the awareness that the woman has her hands full. Sheila feels a pang of pain for Rose and senses that this must have been a painful moment for her.

The pang Sheila felt is typical of the way in which women friends can feel so connected that at times it is as if one is in the other's shoes. This empathic connection is a common feature of women's psychology. A woman's emotional tentacles seek out the precipices in life's emotional terrain. Her receptivity and responsiveness to that terrain feeds her and those around her and gives them an emotional base. Thus Sheila sensed Rose's pain. Without anything being said or indicated by Rose, Sheila was acutely aware that for Rose seeing young children was poignant. In her awareness Sheila actually *felt* Rose's pain. For a brief moment there were no boundaries between them. During a silent moment they shared an intense communication.

Actually, all three women—one a complete stranger—shared a similar connection just moments before. As they exchanged glances there was a complex communication that said, "We know the pleasure you must feel with your two sweet children and we know the stress and pressure you feel in keeping this whole little scene together." The stranger felt understood, appreciated, proud, and supported by the two women at the next table.

Sheila and Rose not only saw the other woman's situation, but for a split second, knew it as if from the inside. When Sheila and Rose left the restaurant, Sheila began a new conversation asking Rose if it was difficult for her to see other women with young children. The two friends, arm in arm, continued their caring and deeply intimate conversation.

Sheila, like other women, has developed emotional antennae. From early on in her life she was directed to be aware of the feelings and needs of others. Her experience of herself when anyone else was around was Sheila in relation to *other*. Knowing what someone else is feeling without their needing to articulate it was one of the first lessons she absorbed as a girl. The more finely tuned in she is to the needs of others, the more highly developed are her skills of intuition. Women's antennae allow them to set people at ease in their discomfort, avoid topics of discussion that cause embarrassment, blush as another person feels shame or humiliation, give a compliment to a near stranger that hits the right spot, tell a funny story when the social situation requires lightening up.

Our upbringing as girls prepares us to be receptive, giving, thoughtful, kind, solicitous; to take account of one another; to see things from the other person's point of view; to feel ourselves in another person's shoes. But these are not simple lessons we learn like algebraic formulas or our times table; they are rather the grammar of women's emotional experience, the internal declensions that organize our relationships to other and self. Within this language, we absorb the emotional grammar, the psychological laws of women's culture, which are every bit as explicit and particular as the cockney language is an encoded expression of the social heritage of London working class culture.

In absorbing the emotional imperatives that are to be women's way of being, we learn not only to be giving, intuitive, receptive, caring, empathic, we learn too that it is ungrammatical to be separate, initiating, autonomous, and self-defined. These ways of being are not considered desirable in girls. Independence, adventurousness, a concern for self are not values that are proudly developed in girls. For that matter, girls who grow up to be independent women are considered freakish in one way or another; they are regarded as brash, spinsterish, sad, selfish, or castrating. They evoke our sympathy or distaste. Their personalities are out of kilter with how we see femininity. We may admire the young woman surgeon for her confidence and ability, but if she devotes herself entirely to her work and remains single, by the time she is in her forties we may feel uneasy, threatened, and somewhat perplexed. We assume that she is odd. Even if it is evident that she is happy, and even if we defend her choices and are inspired by her courage, we can't help feel some discomfort for her. For even today, in the midst of expanding our ideas of what are appropriate behaviors and feelings for women, a woman who resolutely goes her own way jolts us. Deeply etched into our very identity are the grammatically correct ways of being (i.e., psychologically attached) and the grammatically incorrect ways of being (i.e., psychologically separate) women.

In short, girls grow up learning that knowing what others want, caring for them, and being attached to others is the right way to organize their lives. They must create a selfhood dependent on connecting to others. Taking the initiative and seeking a separate identity is wrong unless it comes second. This doesn't mean that girls and women aren't attracted to what is "wrong" (for they are); it doesn't mean that girls and women don't desire autonomy and separateness (for they do); it means rather that their attempts to achieve it are extremely fraught, loaded with guilt and confusion.

Women's desire for love, acceptance, and support from each other is derived from the complex heritage and potential of our first relationship with a woman. For all of us raised in the current style of Western family life, the relationship with mother birthed us physically and emotionally, gave us our first experiences with love and need, disappointment and hurt. Its emotional legacy is etched in the deepest recesses of our hearts. It is the guide and foundation for our future relationships. It sets up needs, ways of being, ways of loving, expectations, and hopes. We have to examine that original mother-daughter relationship in order to understand its legacy. We have to understand what needs it made permissible, and what needs were made inadmissible. We have to understand the texture and feeling of it. We have to understand the particular merged attachment that characterized it before we can grasp both the love and the disappointment, the hope and the hurt that exist in adult women's relationships.

Our inner security as individuals, the enthusiasm or fear with which we engage in new relationships, the possibilities we have imagined for ourselves and the life we have made for ourselves has much to do with what was experienced and conveyed in that first important relationship. And that very first relationship, from its inception, is both an enabling and a disabling one. It is a relationship that is characterized by merger. It is a relationship in which the attachment experienced by mother as well as daughter is both blissful and problematic.

The mother-child relationship is at once a private and public relationship. It is the relationship that nourishes and protects us, while introducing us and preparing us for the social world and its responsibilities. In this sense infancy and childhood are not cozy stages divorced from the wider culture, but developmental stages shaped by the social practices of a given culture. The expectations of social laws, which mothers convey to us, imprint the very intimacy of the mother-child relationship. A mother tries to prepare her daughter to harmoniously live as an individual and take her place in the world.

The social context of the mother-daughter relationship is an important key to explaining not only the bittersweet nature of that relationship but its impact on adult women's relationships. As we understand what could and could not happen for our mothers in their lifetime, as we understand what could and could not happen in our relationships with our mothers, we can begin to understand the forces operating in our current woman-to-woman relationships.

When we leave our mother's womb, we live in a cocooned state with her. Before a baby "knows" itself as a person with a distinct inside and outside, before it can distinguish itself from the people and objects around it, it exists in a merged state with mother. Just as before birth, the infant lives within the actual boundaries of the mother's body, after birth it lives within the mother's psychological boundaries. The mother establishes the psychological milieu that the two inhabit. More precisely, the aspects of the mother's life that concern caring for the infant, and the entire life of the infant fall within this psychological framework.

We tend to romanticize infancy. We imagine an enraptured mother with a baby at the breast. Developmental psychologists describe this as a time when a mother is "given over" to caring for her baby. Almost as though there was nothing separating the two of them, a mother feels merged with the baby, feels whatever holding, feeding, warmth, and so on the baby wants and effortlessly makes the necessary adjustments to maintain its well-being. She guides its psychological development from infantile dependency to subjectivity (separation-individuation[7]). The mother, as a separate person, with her own needs, distinct from the baby, is not in view. In this role, she is only a person who perfectly meets the needs of her infant.

But this idealized picture of a mother effortlessly responding to her baby's every wish and relating appropriately to the developmental stage, conceals a much more complex situation. However in tune a mother may be with her baby, the mothering person is also an individual with needs of her own. Her needs are not excluded from the mother-daughter relationship, they are brought to it and become part of it.

Thus, sensing an infant's need and responding to it is not automatic. The responses themselves are highly affected by the mother's emotional makeup, which, in turn, is determined by the complex of her economic, psychological, and social circumstances. The infant's needs and initiatives invariably evoke some complicated feelings in the mother, which are then expressed by inconsistency in the relating. At times, a mother can respond selflessly to the needs and initiatives of this little girl and she soothes, comforts, encourages, delights in, and loves her effortlessly. The little girl shows her pleasure and her satisfactions, she beams back a smile, a look of contentment that gives the mother a good feeling about herself that is reflected back and forth between the two of them. But often a mother has difficulty with her daughter's expression of need and this easy relating is disrupted. The mother who continually restrains both her own needs for emotional nurturance and her own initiatives is unable to respond to her daughter in an open and generous way. Her responses to her daughter are characterized by annoyance and withdrawal, leaving the daughter confused and rejected. A chain reaction occurs in which the child's need (whether it be for contact and holding, or for support—showing independence or initiative) is ignored, misinterpreted, mismatched by the mother's response and creates in the daughter an uncertainty, an insecurity about herself, her needs, and her desires.

The emotional ambience of the merged attachment, then, contains these contradictory aspects. The relationship is at once a soothing, safe protective environment and an utterly disappointing, frightening, painful place where all can be lost. Mother, caught up in her own internal drama, cannot help but respond inconsistently to her daughter's needs. The daughter, however, has to make sense of her mother's variable responses to her needs.

Of course this phenomenon, the inconsistency in the merged attachment, and the confusion created in the child about which needs and initiatives are sanctioned and which are not, is a feature of all mother-child relationships. But the child's gender is intrinsic to the particular character and shape of the inconsistency and how the mother sees (projects) herself in her child and identifies with the various needs the child is expressing.

A mother sees a son and a daughter differently. Mother can see her son as "other," as different; the gender difference provides a clear-cut boundary between them. He is he and she is she. Differentiation by gender is not present with a daughter. Throughout the many phases of her daughter's life, a mother watches and is continually reminded of her own girlhood; her own childhood wishes and desires, as well as the restrictions she experienced. Images of her own childhood insinuate themselves into the interaction between her and her daughter. In other words, *when she looks at her daughter she sees herself.*

What are the psychological implications for daughters? What most mothers have great difficulty in sanctioning in their daughters are their daughters' needs for dependency and their needs to initiate. In raising a daughter, a mother is inclined to curb her daughter's needs for nurturance. She learns to limit her own initiatives insofar as they interrupt her availability to others. Like her mother, she will come to understand that autonomy is not a route to feminine selfhood. Selfhood will be found through her identification and adjustment to the needs of others. A critical expectation, established by social law, and passed on from mother to daughter, is that the daughter's selfhood must develop in a relational context. Like her mother, she should find "herself" and know "herself" through responsiveness to others. *A woman's subjectivity is relational.*

Other psychological expectations are conveyed by mother to daughter, for mother brings her needs into the relationship with her daughter. Foremost is the mother's need for attachment. Her connection to her child, like any other intimate connection, contains a crucial piece of her psychological selfhood. Her identity is entwined with this and she brings the urgency of *her* need for connection into the relationship with her daughter. Thus the period of infantile dependency is marked not only by the daughter's psychological merger and need of mother *but with the mother's need for psychological merger with her daughter.* Parenthetically, the mother conveys to her daughter the sense that this is how she too will find herself.

And just like mother, the daughter seeks a sense of self through connection, without which there is an underlying insecurity. For without connection, a feminine identity is at risk. Attachment to and concern for others becomes her guide. The daughter is taught to interpret her own feelings in this light. She begins to identify the satisfying of others' needs and complying with others as *a need of her own.* She develops the capacity to feel herself into others' experience to know what they are wanting and needing.

But her sensitivity to others' needs does not simply come from being watchful and solicitous. It is because her own needs are unmet or distorted that she becomes attuned to neediness in others. Her own deep neediness invokes in her a capacity to identify with, emotionally register, and respond to the neediness of others.

This capacity to feel herself into someone else's experience and the impulse to take account of others' feelings—such central features of woman-to-woman relating—at the same time produces an insecurity about other feelings. She becomes curiously inexperienced and embarrassed by her own needs, despite her expertise in heeding the emotional needs of others. Desires that arise in her, such as a wish to be "free," on her own, unencumbered by the emotional demands of others, desires that conflict with the merged attachment, confuse her. Desires for self-nurturing or desires that compete with her caring for others, are perplexing because she does not receive consistent or unambiguous support for them. She juggles them internally, at one moment repressing them, at another seeking to express them. Over time, she becomes fearful of wishing to pursue her own initiatives. Desires she may experience for autonomy, for separateness, frighten her. Because of this fear, she is unable to leave the state of merged attachment, which feels safe and known. It is as though she faces a dreadful choice. She can either exist as a lone individual unconnected to others or be trapped in a nexus of cloying attachments. She does not believe that she can have both her attachments and her autonomy. She has no experience of this.

She has learned directly and indirectly in this first important relationship with her mother, that attachment to others—a prerequisite of survival—depends upon two features: the repression of her embryonic self (containing her need for dependency and autonomy), and an almost compulsive concern for others. Thus attachment, as she knows it, is itself problematic. For it is characterized by repression and merger. It goes hand in hand with the loss of a personal identity.

As we can see, the shared gender of mother and daughter has many implications for woman-to-woman relating. The mother's need for attachment, combined with her identification with her daughter, creates a fusion between the two of them (a merged attachment). The mother is not separate from her daughter and as her daughter expresses her needs, the mother experiences them *with* her, almost as though they were *her own*. She feels them too.

The daughter has an equivalent experience as she grows into womanhood. Not only does she retain her mother's presence inside her, not only does she feel acutely aware of her mother's neediness, not only does she feel responsible for maintaining the attachment she feels her mother needs, but, unconsciously, she will bring this responsibility with her into her future relationships with both lovers and friends.

In adult relationships, she is searching to find herself. But because the only mechanism she has for doing so is through merging and identifying with others, she comes to these relationships with emotional malleability. She comes with her emotional antennae ready to tune into the needs of the other. She is ready to adjust herself, deny herself, indeed lose herself (in order to find her self) in the attachment. But this process means that she loses sight of her own separate needs and desires. A search begins to find them in the other. She may no longer know what she wants in a clear way and looks to the other to provide an answer. She is dutifully concerned with the desires of her lover or friend, and gauges herself accordingly. She knows no other form of intimate attachment. Her adult relationships are woven with the threads of merged attachments. But these threads are not simply connective. They are constricting and binding. In the attachment, individual needs or individual development are a threat and so they are resisted. The merger that serves to shore up a shaky identity simultaneously precludes separate development. Thus relations based on merger mean that often women are bound to one another in a restricting way. Without realizing it, in bonding together to find strength, they can feel severely limited.

This phenomenon of merged attachment is the fabric out of which adult female friendships are fashioned. Like a patchwork quilt, dark and light, patterned and plain, soft and rough materials play off one another creating an intricate whole. In the merged attachment, the different strands are composed of contradictory feelings, injunctions, and longings. If we follow one piece of the pattern we can see how women are able to intimately connect, to care for one another in the most exquisitely sensitive of ways; another issues the injunction to relate to and serve others. If we focus on another piece of the pattern we see how women unwittingly hold themselves and each other back; how their fear of separation leads them to sabotage their own and their dearest friends' efforts to achieve autonomy. Indirectly and unknowingly, women can restrain their friends; they can discourage their efforts toward separateness and success. Fear of abandonment, or the threat to abandon another, signal to each other that attempts toward separation are dangerous.

As we make out the pattern of yet another patch, we see how with one another, women attempt to repair painful aspects of their relationships with their mothers to alleviate the pain and disappointment they carry; to find a relationship that gives them love while allowing them to be separate. Close by, another patch shows the fear, the hesitation, the disbelief that they can have such a connection; that they will be allowed to be separate and still receive love and acceptance. As we focus on the different patches that make up the whole we see that *women's psychology is currently constructed in such a way that her capacities to be close and giving and her fear of separation are psychically inseparable.*

The Giver

Roberta is an administrative nurse in a large New York hospital. She is responsible for the services for all postoperative patients in a particular wing. Doctors, other nurses, family members, general staff, all regard Roberta as a source of information and organization. Her day is filled from early morning to early evening with answering questions, giving instructions and information, relaying messages, solving the problems that continually arise, and generally maintaining order. Everyone thinks Roberta is fantastic. She does her job so well that even in the hectic, frenzied pace of the floor, all who come into contact with her are aware of her competence, her concern, her dedication. The staff know that without Roberta, the wing would dissolve into utter chaos. Roberta is single and lives alone. Most weekday evenings she returns home after work, and noshes her way through several hours in front of the television. As she goes to bed, she berates herself for not doing anything worthwhile that evening and not keeping to her diet. On evenings when she goes out with a friend she enjoys listening to her news and commiserating or offering advice. She rarely talks about herself but she enjoys the shared time and feels sustained by the contact and the knowledge that she has given something to her friend.

Roberta knows only too well how to be on the giving end of a relationship. She feels comfortable and safe. She gets satisfaction from accomplishing the multitude of tasks at work and being able to wisely counsel her friends. We all know a Roberta, a woman who always has something to give and seemingly little need of her own. But does she truly have little need? What are Roberta's needs?

The truth is that Roberta's needs are in the shadow of her giving. One need not look too far; just as a shadow follows immediately in the path of its object, Roberta's needs are connected to her giving.

Central to Roberta's giving is her own emotional hunger. Confronted with a person's needs, little or big, she becomes uncomfortable because her own neediness is touched. As she gives to the other, unconsciously she is attempting to satisfy her own unmet need. Part of her ability to know, to intuit, to read the needs of others comes from her own yearning for that very same care. Roberta does not feel entitled to bring her own needs to a relationship. She is ashamed of them and afraid of her insatiability. She has no confidence that she (and her needs) have a beginning and an end. It is as though she has no boundary, no knowledge of a defined self. This is the cost, the damage of living in the shadow of others and being such a good giver. Although she gives all the time, she is continually in retreat from friendship to which she can bring her inner self. She is disabled in her relationships with others.

Roberta, like others, learned from very early in her life to curb her own neediness. The consequence is that her own self-development is channeled toward the care of others and the search for her own self in others. When little girls make demands on their own behalf they often face disapproval. The little girl's wants are considered selfish and unattractive. In an attempt to hide her demands, whether for individuation and initiation or for cuddling and containment, a part of a girl's developing personality becomes buried. We have come to call this buried part the little-girl inside each woman. Outwardly she appears to be a person who stands on her own two feet, is a competent person on whom others can depend both emotionally and physically. And indeed she is. But inside part of her still longs for continued attachment. She has come to dislike and fear this part of herself, which continually reminds her that, she too, has needs.

Delegation to caretaker of others and the denial of the essential foods for self-development is part of women's psychological legacy. Many a woman has felt inner emptiness and the sense of emotional deprivation that springs from the inconsistent caring she has received. This emotional deprivation often translates as compulsive giving, depression, hopelessness, chronic resentment, or rage. In the presence of others, she spontaneously gives them attention and responds to their needs. Indeed, that capacity keeps her going and gives her a good feeling about herself. Roberta is a perhaps extreme example of someone who finds it very hard to reveal that she has needs. She is deeply ashamed of these needs and unused to addressing them directly. Indeed, she may be conscious of them only when a crisis forces them to the surface. The only hint to others and herself is her preoccupation with weight and dieting, a context in which she can talk about how unhappy she is and how out of control she feels around food. But most of the time, as she sits with a friend or a lover, although she feels vaguely unsatisfied, she may be too cut off to even realize how much she yearns for them to reach out to her, to see inside her, to accept and understand her neediness, to give to her. When she is in crisis and people do rally around her, she feels humiliated and hates herself for exposing what feels like unreasonable needs.

Roberta's story is not that uncommon. Closeness with other women in adult friendships stimulates and recreates the desire for a merged attachment. For in this merged attachment a woman finds a self. Equally, however, the little-girl inside longs for a different kind of attachment, one that acknowledges her past needs and restrictions and addresses her present needs, thus allowing her to mature. If this could happen, the woman would no longer feel desperate and insatiable. Her personality would not have to be split but could become integrated. She would develop a more secure subjectivity. A sense of selfhood based on *having* rather than deprivation. A sense of selfhood based on entitlement rather than denial. A sense of selfhood that is bounded rather than compulsively relational. Although it is not possible to do away with the hurt of our childhood, it is possible to acknowledge and understand that hurt. By coming to grips with the past, it becomes possible to digest the nurturance that is available in our current relationships. If we can acknowledge the pain, the hurt, and the disappointment of the past, if we can accept that the deprivation wasn't our fault, current and future relationships need not be defined and burdened by the need to repair or repeat the past. What can emerge are relationships between equal adults who each have needs, rather than paradigms of mother-child relationships in which one is the apparent giver and the other the apparent receiver.

But this is the precise area of difficulty for women, for we have little confidence that relationships and a selfhood not built on a version of the mother-child merger (in which the compulsive attending to needs of the other, the repression of one's own initiatives, and the denial of difference are endemic) can survive.

One of the unfortunate implications of a woman's identification with the needs of the other is that sometimes it matches the other's experience, but often it does not. Identifying is a particular kind of giving where one unconsciously puts oneself in the place of another. Women's capacity to identify is almost automatic. As we listen to a woman friend telling us about a problem or dilemma we *feel* with her, as if it were happening to us.

This kind of emotional response, this capacity to feel what another is feeling, is like second nature, but holds the risk of misinterpreting the other's experience. Identification is also the search for self, and a woman's malleable boundaries create confusion about where she ends and another person begins. While it appears to bring us close to another person, identification simultaneously distorts the contact and results in inappropriate relating.

Thus, because of women's psychological history, the nature of the mother-daughter merged attachment, and the intensity of need that is brought to women's friendships, women often identify with one another rather than see the other's experience and empathize with it.

In other words, there is a confusion between empathy and identification which, though similar, are different in important ways. Empathy is the ability to imagine or think about another person's condition, taking on the feelings of the other only fleetingly. Empathy is a conscious process whereby one attempts to understand the experience of another. One remains detached and outside the situation while deeply involved with the other person in the process of relating. The ability to feel empathy is a most essential skill to bring to one's friendships, to parenting, to intimate relationships. To be with other people authentically, that is, to see them as they are, for who they are in their own right, to respond to what they need and not to see them as we need or imagine them to be, is no easy feat. This ability depends on an awareness of self as a unique, defined, autonomous individual who relies and depends upon connections to other separate, defined, autonomous people.

As we have seen, women's easy connections occur in

an emotional field that has both negative and positive currents. While one surges with our craving for love, for understanding, for recognition, for sympathy, for support, for commiseration, it is entwined with another surge, negatively charged. The negative current disrupts apparently easy connections by emitting a whole set of interferences—a constricting field of social and psychological mandates through which women prohibit one another from certain kinds of self-expression. The combined forces inform the texture of the relationships and the often unspoken and unconscious agreements made within friendships.

As the following chapters show, tensions and unconscious agreements between women are restraining. We are so accustomed to restricting ourselves and one another that we are unpracticed in supporting ourselves and one another in the struggle toward differentiation. We barely believe differentiation is possible and even if it is, we conceive of it as too threatening unless we all embark on it at the same time, in concert. We long to emulate women who manage to break free of the merged attachment but our fear turns into envy and we castigate them for stepping out of line and deserting us. We feel our inadequacy and can't imagine how other women are adequate and we turn our upset into competition and self-hate. We feel guilty that we impede one another and furious at being impeded. We are angry because we long to stay in the merged attachment and we are angry because we wish to be separate. We project onto other women our fears, which are then mirrored back because other women have them too. We look for an all-embracing, loving friendship or lover but we anticipate rejection and restriction. We have a deep and passionate attachment with one another that is at once holding and binding. In order to achieve more empathic relating, in order to give and receive genuine support from one another, women need to move out of the constricting aspects of merged attachment into an attachment based on separateness.

Chapter 4

Abandonment

Rena and Elise are twenty-eight-year-old lab technicians working in Edinburgh, who became friends through work three years ago. When they first met, Rena was living with Adam. When Rena and Adam split up, Rena felt depressed, lonely, and bereft. Over lunch she would talk to Elise about the kinds of things she was going through, her unfinished anger toward Adam, her fears of being alone, her doubts about ever finding another man. Elise was single herself and had gone through several separations from intimate relationships, so she was able to lend a sympathetic ear. She knew the kinds of things that Rena was feeling and could commiserate easily. The two women began to spend more and more time together, going to movies, out to dinner, shopping, and generally developing a close companionship. They phoned each other in the evenings to chat, saying that they would see one another the next day at work.

Generally marriages and sexual relationships provide the kind of relationship that Rena and Elise developed. We know and accept that couples are dependent upon one another in all kinds of ways. And even though we know that close women friends are emotionally dependent upon one another, we rarely acknowledge how important these ties are. When women are not involved in couple relationships, when they live alone or perhaps are raising children on their own, intimacy with a girlfriend may be their most significant adult emotional tie. It is estimated that sixty percent of women in the United States in their thirties are single. Like Rena and Elise, single women friends speak to each other daily, go to social events together, plan their vacations together. In our culture, friendship is often allocated a secondary position while only marriages and sexual relationships are seen as truly significant. However, this contrasts with the experience of many women whose friendships function—for long periods of time—as primary relationships. In such a situation, when one of the women becomes involved in a sexual or romantic relationship, the other can feel painfully abandoned.

For weeks Rena was attracted to a new biochemist at work. She and Elise giggled about it at lunch and plotted strategies for Rena to meet him. For the most part, Elise was not disturbed by these conversations because their various interests in different people had always been a part of their friendship. But when Rena phoned Elise and excitedly announced that she had done it, she had gone up to John and introduced herself, Elise felt a pang of upset. She listened to every detail of the encounter, asked questions, and shared in her friend's delight. But when she hung up, she burst into tears. She felt a terrible loss and she felt frightened. She tried to calm herself by telling herself that she was silly, that this degree of upset

74

made no sense, but she could not rid herself of these feelings.

Because women derive so much of their identity and sense of well-being through attachment, and because women's friendships contain a merged attachment, a friend with whom one has made a significant attachment serves almost as a part of the self. The sharing of time, activities, aspirations, pleasures, and pains transforms an individual sense of inner emptiness into one of rooted-ness and connectedness. A shift in a friendship that in-volves or presages loss, may entail two disturbing and simultaneous results. On the one hand, a woman may feel somewhat disoriented, unconnected, and at sea, as though she has lost part of herself. On the other hand, because the underlying emotional connection in female friendships resonates with aspects of the mother-daugh-ter relationship, the loss or shifting of a close friendship can stir up, consciously or unconsciously, the pain and anger women can feel about disappointing aspects of their relationship with their mothers.

For each friend involved, woman-to-woman relation-ships duplicate aspects of the mother-daughter rela-tionship and simultaneously extend the promise to re-pair some of the hurt and difficulties of the original rela-tionship. Consequently, in adult female friendships we frequently observe an unconscious wish to merge with the other person, to be mothered and cared for, to receive the nurturance that they continue to crave. Each woman may unconsciously look to the other one to provide whatever she didn't get from her mother; she may de-pend on her friend for support and encouragement and approval and because she may need this so very badly, she may be in acute pain when the friend becomes involved in another close relationship. She experiences both the actual loss (of certain aspects of her relationship with her friend) and the feelings it triggers about losing the intimacy and closeness she once had (or had longed to have) with her mother. The pain evoked may confuse her, for she may be unaware of her continuing search and need for a merged attachment with her women friends.

Rena and Elise's friendship underwent a profound change. When Rena started dating John, she became very caught up in the excitement that a new love affair inevitably produces. Although Rena and Elise still continued to see one another every day at work and still had lunch together on most weekdays, Rena was less available. Her weekend time was now almost entirely devoted to John and although she made obvious efforts to be sensitive to Elise, to be sure that they continued to see one another, nonetheless their time together had changed dramatically.

Elise could not escape the deeply painful feelings of abandonment. Weekends became difficult. She made what often seemed like desperate efforts to spend time with her other friends, but many Saturday nights she sat alone in front of the television. But it wasn't simply loneliness that Elise was experiencing; she felt depressed, hopeless, and disconnected. Even when she went out with John and Rena, she was unhappy and felt awkward, pathetic, and out of place. When she was having a good time with them, enjoying a film or a meal, she couldn't escape the yearning for an attachment. No longer so central to Rena's life, Elise felt cut loose, detached, and as though she had lost a part of herself. As Rena's availability diminished, Elise became acutely aware of her emotional dependency on their relationship. She now had no one to bring her dependency to.

Whereas everyone commiserates and recognizes the loneliness that is part of a breakup when a woman loses a boyfriend or a man loses his partner, few people take account of the loneliness and discomfort a woman feels when her relationship with a close girlfriend changes. Nobody rushes round with hot dinners or evening entertainments—it would strike us all as very odd if anyone did. But the dependency girlfriends develop toward one another is not trivial. The loss of a girlfriend through geography or through a change in her personal circumstances is significant. It does hurt. It does shake each woman up inside. It can be as severe an emotional wallop as a serious shift in a sexual relationship. It can render one temporarily fragile in similar ways. For all these reasons we need to pay attention to the shifts and losses in significant relationships between women. Acknowledging the real adjustments that have to be made and the loss that is felt is an important first step. If that can occur, then the complex of identity issues that may have been camouflaged in the merged attachment can emerge and be sorted through.

Elise needed to be able to accept that she was upset; to give up the notion that she shouldn't be upset. If, together, Elise and Rena had been able to acknowledge the impact of Rena's love affair on their friendship, Elise might have felt less alone in her grief. She would still have had to bear the loss of a special intimacy, but the emotional gutting she experienced, the feeling of being detached, would have been mitigated by Rena's support and understanding.

To provide this kind of emotional support, Rena

would have had to be able to acknowledge and override any guilt she had about being in a sexual relationship. It may seem strange that "getting for oneself" engenders guilt, but in so many instances, as in hers, this *is* what occurs. Rena was subconsciously aware that she had abandoned Elise, and part of her felt deeply guilty for having done so. She couldn't bear to see Elise's pain because she felt she had caused it. Her guilt interfered with her ability to stay emotionally connected (on a new basis) and in touch with Elise's needs.

The struggle that each woman faced was to resist both feeling guilty toward one another and withdrawing from the friendship. It was true that the existing equilibrium was disrupted, but that did not mean they couldn't find a new basis to connect and support one another.

The line between a genuine abandonment and an imagined one can be irrelevant in terms of the strength of feeling it stirs up. Because women's needs for one another are so strong, and yet there is a taboo against openly accepting that dependency, our antennae are alert to the potential abandonment in a wide variety of situations.

Margaret and Adeline are social workers and best friends. They've known each other since college and have been through marriages, the arrival of children, graduate school, and career development side by side. At forty-two, after her second child started kindergarten, Margaret decided to go back to school and enrolled in an analytic institute that would enable her to enter practice in psychotherapy. Adeline told her that she thought this was wonderful, that Margaret was brave to try something new at this point. Each time they spoke, Adeline made a point of asking Margaret about her progress toward acceptance and was very supportive of her best friend. But alongside her genuine interest and support, Adeline was upset. She was worried that Margaret's move to a new professional level would take Margaret away from her. She hated herself for being so shaken and upset and thought that these feelings meant that she was truly a selfish person and a despicable friend. She tried to reassure herself that this change needn't disrupt the friendship. She reminded herself that she chose to remain in casework and not psychotherapy, and that Margaret's choice to do something different didn't mean that her own work was useless or less valuable. But she was stunned by the strength of her feelings. Margaret's proposed professional advancement aroused in her the same kinds of feelings she had experienced when her daughter marched off to kindergarten; on that occasion, Adeline had sat in the car and cried.

The difficult feelings that Adeline was aware of in herself are extremely common today. Her best friend's efforts to develop herself stirred up in Adeline the feeling that she was being abandoned. Her upset illustrates the ways in which the merged attachment, so often a feature of women's friendships, creates for women a glue for their own sense of self. When that merger is broken, the adhesive dissolves and the woman feels shaken up inside. She questions whether her own arrangements hold up, whether they are enough. Before, Adeline had felt perfectly satisfied with her own work. Now, Margaret had chosen to leave the same work and move on to something new and Adeline felt as if she was left with nothing.

Margaret, in her turn, had a complementary set of difficult feelings to confront. Margaret was anxious about telling Adeline of her decision to pursue further training, fearing that somehow this news would be upsetting. Thus, she discussed it almost apologetically, providing a long list of justifications. In describing this growth-producing decision to her best friend, she belittled its very meaning. Unconsciously, she hoped that if she made it appear to be less than it was, less desirable, less than what it really meant to her, it would not threaten or upset Adeline.

Both Margaret and Adeline believe that their self-development will threaten other women, although they were never taught explicitly to think this. Every woman is aware of the potential she has to arouse feelings of abandonment or betrayal in others when she acts autonomously and this awareness may cause a pervading sense of the danger and impermissibility of her actions. Not only is a woman aware that her activities and desires can cause pain to others, she may herself suffer stress about acting on her desires, believing that there is something wrong with wanting to take initiatives.

It becomes understandable that women have enormous difficulty approaching these issues straightforwardly. While both Margaret and Adeline were social workers, part of the security in their attachment was based on a commonality, a sameness that allowed them to rely on their connection without question. The connection meant a lot to both of them; they had given each other so much. In fact, it was partly through the love and support that Margaret had experienced in the relationship that she had come to a more expansive view of herself, which now included feeling entitled enough to pursue a new career direction. But this very love and caring that flowed between them, on which Margaret flourished, precipitated the inevitable adjustments in their relationship. Margaret's career change signified a psychological differentiation: a break in the merged attachment.

Adeline worried that there might be a threat to the relationship, that Margaret would develop new interests which she couldn't share, that perhaps Margaret would get closer to another woman with whom she would share the new common experience. She couldn't securely hold onto the real attachment that she and Margaret shared. Breaking the merged attachment, which was an aspect of their relationship, made her uneasy. She felt abandoned. Consciously she knew that their friendship would survive the change, but unconsciously she feared that their love and caring could not survive their separation. Margaret, meanwhile, felt that she was doing something impermissible; she couldn't rid herself of the feeling that she was betraying her friend. She feared she would lose Adeline's support unless she stayed a social worker (i.e., merged with her). In chapter 8, we look at how Adeline and Margaret talked about their fears with one another and the ways they were able to support each another in breaking their merged attachment while still staying close and connected.

Christine and Andrea are best friends. They are both single and in their thirties. Christine is a kindergarten teacher and Andrea is going to law school. They phone each other every night to check in and commiserate about the day's tiring events and spend most of their weekend time together. A strong theme in their relationship is the support they give one another around the dissatisfactions in their lives. Usually one or the other is in a bad state, upset, or in a rage about something that has just happened to her at work or in another relationship. Each wholeheartedly engages in the trials and tribulations of the other and offers unconditional support to her friend's position. It is as if they are on a seesaw on which first one is up and the other down and then vice versa.

Christine and Andrea have a system worked out between them. They are locked in rage together and although each apparently supports the other, the support simultaneously conceals a process in which they are helping one another cover up the tremendous pain each feels alongside the rage. As one jumps to the other's defense she is unconsciously identifying with the pain, the hurt, the deprivation. But for each of them anger serves as a protection against the deeper, more painful feelings. They link arms through their anger and as they commiserate, their joint anger creates a barricade against these painful feelings. They share a difficulty in exposing need or hurt directly, and their identification and merged attachment serves to conceal their vulnerability.

During Andrea's last year in law school she met and became friendly with Joan. Joan was a self-confident, contented woman who liked to enjoy herself. Andrea was drawn to her. At this point, having nearly completed law school, Andrea herself felt a growing confidence and optimism about life that was new to her. Each time she went out with Joan she enjoyed herself. They went to shows, movies, dinners, and always had a good time together.

Meanwhile, Andrea began to feel irritated with Christine. Christine's never-ending sagas of mistreatment and victimization were becoming annoying. The more aware Andrea became of Christine's negativity, the less she could tolerate it. Gradually, she distanced herself more and more until she had completely altered what had previously been a close friendship.

Christine, on the other hand, felt devastated. She was on an emotional roller coaster. First, she felt jealous of Joan. She found herself criticizing Joan to Andrea and was aware that she felt very competitive toward her for Andrea's affection. Then, she felt desperate that her efforts to get Andrea's care didn't work. What had happened? Andrea had always supported and given attention to her problems, why was she abandoning her now? Each time she spoke to Andrea about how depressed she was feeling, Andrea seemed to move further and further away. Christine was consumed with feelings of competition toward Joan, envy of the good times that Andrea was having, and painful abandonment and aloneness.

Christine and Andrea's attachment was built on sameness and commiseration about not having. When Andrea began to feel differently, when she liked the feelings of having and wanting more, the friendship shattered. They did not know how to change together or how to tolerate the differences that were emerging between them. They didn't know how to talk about the kinds of feelings they each were experiencing. Andrea felt that she was betraying Christine when she told her that she was having a good time. Christine felt abandoned by Andrea. The differences and the inability to talk about what was happening formed a widening gulf. Andrea felt guilty and intimidated. Christine was hurt and furious. As in so many situations where differences between women friends cannot be talked about or accepted, the situation between them became intolerable. The only resolution was to sever the ties. Andrea was left feeling guilty, Christine was left feeling bereft.

The kinds of feelings that Christine, Andrea, Rena, Elise, Margaret, and Adeline experienced vis-à-vis one another are often exacerbated in a group situation, making it even harder to understand the root causes of discomfort and dissension within groups.

When Laurie, the thirty-year-old founder and director of a women's dance company from Southern California, went on pregnancy leave the other company members felt abandoned. They went through a painful process in trying to come to terms with the prospect of Laurie's year-long absence. At first they felt extremely nervous about forthcoming performances. They felt incapable of putting it all together. They felt angry about being left. After the first couple of months, as they began to realize that they really had to and could take responsibility for running the company, a kind of disparaging contempt for Laurie set in. Their insecurity about running the company was suppressed, their former admiration for Laurie's capabilities was receding, and there was a general denial of the early achievements of the company.

The emotional drama that unfolded becomes understandable when we remember that women's relationships with one another are loaded with a psychological significance quite outside the apparently straightforward professional responsibilities they share. We shall explore some of these themes in subsequent chapters, but for now it is important to see how the feelings of abandonment created havoc in the dance company.

The group as a whole related to Laurie as though she

was the mother who would and should take care of them, never leave them, provide support and encouragement and a happy environment for them to work in. In transferring these kinds of hopes to the director, the group members psychologically relinquished some of their own capacity to fend for themselves. There was a conflict between acknowledging their own competence and their continuing needs. Like many adult women today, these women had a strong desire to be cared for. At the same time, they all felt somewhat ashamed of such wishes and so they were never discussed or openly acknowledged. Although the group was composed of independent-minded, competent, and talented women, their outward confidence and high level of professional skill sat side by side with vulnerable and shaky feelings.

They felt this way for all the previously discussed reasons that women today are inclined to feel unsure and fraudulent. If anything, dance training compounds those feelings since it in no way addresses the kinds of social and psychological pressures that women experience as they struggle to gain recognition. Dancers are always expected to make themselves even better and enjoy little sense of having achieved a position of being good enough, adequate, sufficient. For these women, maintaining their status as professional dancers was itself a pressure. They were always vulnerable and were expected to be utterly dedicated and perfectionistic. There was a conflict between their professional and private personas: professionally, they were seen as extremely confident and together; privately, they each had feelings of inadequacy and fraudulence.

Laurie's presence as director had provided each woman with a kind of antidote or safety net against confusing internal feelings. She had been seen as—and to a certain extent had acted as—a parent who had given birth to the group and enabled it to function well. She was confident enough for all of them.

By the time Laurie was about to return to work after her year's absence, the group felt discomfort rather than excitement. There was a fear of reintegrating her. The psychological shifts that the group had experienced in response to being abandoned now stood in the way of letting Laurie back in. The new coherence in the group that had evolved as a result of Laurie's pregnancy leave now depended on her exclusion. In other words, the remaining members had managed the havoc and upset caused by Laurie's departure by bonding together. Of course, this was one of the few options open to them. Because they had felt so insecure and worried about her leaving, the group needed to find a new basis of support and connection with one another. They bonded together in the shared experience of abandonment and the survival of that abandonment. This new merged attachment provided them with some strength and a psychological basis for continuing. Letting Laurie back in, letting themselves once again feel her importance, would reopen the pain of the loss. In this case it was not merely the loss of Laurie for one year, but rather that the loss touched on much deeper feelings of dependency, attachment, and need, for each of the women in the group.

The group had found a solution that sidestepped their feelings toward Laurie. In developing a strategy that kept her out, they denied to themselves their need for her leadership and emotional support. When she returned, there was an uncomfortable period of realignment. Some members yearned for the group to return to the way it had been while others were hostile to Laurie and criticized her new choreographic arrangements in an unhelpful manner. These very different responses both related to the merged attachment that still existed in the group. Those who wanted to nestle cozily back in sought a return to the merger. Those who were fractious were expressing how deserted they had felt when Laurie left. Her pregnancy had ruptured the merger and that was felt by some members, unconsciously, as an attack.

The group was not functioning well and tension permeated work. The company needed to talk about the psychological dimension of Laurie's pregnancy leave and her return. In bringing such issues into the open, less destructive responses could emerge. If the group had found a way to *talk together about,* rather than enacting, their negative and insecure feelings, the dance company as a whole could have found a new basis for being together. Without necessarily understanding all the deep psychological meanings and ramifications, hearing one another's reactions to the new situation and expressing their own would have established a different way of relating. They would have broken into the merged attachment and recreated a supportive work atmosphere on different terms.

It is possible to attribute the difficulties women friends and colleagues have with one another simply to changed circumstances. Of course, as our circumstances develop and change, it may well be that our friends no longer suit us or provide us with the stimulation, pleasure, or support that we need. The friends we have in high school may be different from those friends we seek out in college or in later life. When we change jobs, or move from being single to being a couple or vice versa, we may notice that as our interests change, so do our friends. For many of us, moving on to new things and saying goodbye to old friends is positive, especially where we have felt trapped in relationships that are unbalanced, draining, or only dutiful. It is inevitable that new ventures and growth will mean new friends and the loss of some old ones. Indeed, some might argue that the upsets that Christine, Andrea, Rena, Elise, Margaret, and Adeline felt are just something that they should have been able to take in their stride. We can't, some might say, count on things to stay the same in life; indeed, we would not want them to, and with change come hurdles that just have to be overcome.

But to take this view would be both to underestimate the dependency that exists in women's relationships and to denigrate these women's heartfelt experiences. Of course these hurdles have to be faced and overcome. Some friends need to be given up, and often we have to overcome some guilt to do so. We feel guilt or sadness when we lose a friendship precisely because most friendships are very important to us. They are neither trivial nor stopgap relationships. But when it becomes clear that our interests have become irreconcilable, and one has to say goodbye to a friendship, we often don't know how to do it. We don't have the conventions to handle separations or the endings of love affairs. We can say about a love affair that it was important at the time but it couldn't last. We can savor it and regret that it was limited. But no such language enters discussions on friendship; we either tend to feel guilt that we have abandoned a friend or anger that we have been left. Friendship is not something we pick up and use as a convenience, friends are not irreplaceable and interchangeable, even if, as we have seen, some of the psychological dimensions, especially replays of the mother-daughter relationship, are transferred from relationship to relationship. Each friendship is unique. Just as a love relationship gives something to each lover, changes them, helps them grow and develop in particular ways, friendships between women have a deep effect.

Within friendships women grow, help one another develop confidence, receive love and nurturance, understanding and compassion. Paradoxically, the things women give one another help them to move out of the position of merged attachment. Gaining a stronger self-identity provides a stepping-stone for growth and individuation. But as we have seen with Adeline and Margaret, Christine and Andrea, and with the dance company, a friend's changing circumstances can feel like an abandonment.

There is an ethos within women's relationships—prevalent whether relationships are informed by feminism or not—an ethos that requires staying in the same place together or moving forward together at the same time. In other words, difference cannot be allowed and it is experienced as dangerous and threatening, and invokes feelings of abandonment.

To put it very bluntly, the unspoken bargain between women is that we must all stay the same. If we act on a want, if we differentiate, if we dare to be psychologically separate, we break ranks. We are disrupting the known: the merged attachment.

We can't trust that attachment and closeness can continue from a different basis, for we have no knowledge of it. We are fearful that the identity and strength we gain from self-development will cut us off from our still-needed connections with other women. The urge to stay merged and the urge to separate exist simultaneously and create a tension in women's relationships. Every woman senses that there is a price to pay for self-actualization. It engenders feelings of guilt in oneself while it stirs up feelings of envy, competition, and anger in other women.

Sometimes our friendships can be the repository of our old ways of being. They contain the knowledge of who we were then and who we are now, they provide us with a psychological continuity just as a family provides us with a chronological continuity. Because our friendships can give us so much and help us to change, we do not want to jettison them simply because that change can bring difficulties in its turn. By facing the unconscious fears of abandonment, by allowing one another to grow separately and within the relationship, we build the basis for a new trust within women's relationships.

Chapter 5

Envy

Amy and Lynn are good friends. Amy has been living with Mike for four years and has a year-old baby. Lynn was divorced two years ago and has recently started dating men again. The two women are very involved in each other's lives despite their different situations. Lynn tells Amy all about her various dating pleasures and fiascos and Amy tells Lynn about the newest things the baby accomplished on any given day. One night they are invited to a party to which Lynn brings her newest lover. Amy and Mike have been at the party a while when Lynn and Ron arrive. Amy notices that Lynn looks radiant, sexy, and really happy. She watches as Lynn and Ron do a sexy dance. Amy feels herself sinking. Suddenly she feels fat, she hates her dress, her hair, herself. She is painfully aware of how little she and Mike are connecting. She feels envious and inwardly berates herself for such awful feelings toward her best friend.

The following Sunday, Lynn is visiting Amy. Mike, Amy, Lynn, and little Rosa are sitting at the dining-room table over a lovely brunch spread. Rosa is adorable and Mike and Amy are clearly bursting with delight and pride over their child. Lynn watches the scene and feels despairing. She's thirty-five, without a child and without a relationship that might produce a child. She feels like a failure, she feels alone, and she feels envy toward her best friend, who seems to have it all worked out.

Envy is among the most painful feelings women experience toward other women. It occurs once and causes discomfort. It occurs a second time and the woman tries to avoid or suppress it. The third time, the woman feels persecuted by this unbearable feeling. As we have discussed, with the changes in women's role and women's expectations over the last decade, our awareness of this reaction is on the rise, threatening to disrupt even the best of female friendships.

Envy may be evoked toward only one particular woman, perhaps only in particular situations. In any case, it causes tremendous discomfort and shame. Lynn and Amy each would have given anything *not* to feel the sickness of envy toward each other. Viscerally, each felt as if their very bodies had been taken over by foreign matter. Envy hurts; it breeds distrust, stirs up gruesome fantasies of revenge, and creates distance from a close friend.

Because it is so difficult to express such negative feelings in women's friendships, often the psychological outlet is self-criticism. Amy felt ugly and asexual; Lynn felt like a failure. Each took the unacceptable and distressing feeling and turned it against herself. A negative feeling toward a woman friend is so threatening that we feel safer with the pain of our own self-hatred. The woman feels hurt, pushed out, or angry and assumes that it is she who is faulty or lacking. She tries to change her behavior or her character to prevent a repetition of the unpleasant feelings. When these upsetting feelings rebound forcefully and insistently, she may wish to deflect them by covering them up or turning them into something else. Unused to experiencing these feelings directly, she may be eaten up by them, becoming nervous and anxious and suffering tremendous emotional discomfort and pain.

Amy and Lynn didn't have a simple solution to their discomfort, but they shared the pain and upset rather than turn it into self-denigration. Amy told Lynn how gorgeous she looked and complained about how frumpy she'd been feeling lately. In this way she responded to the part of her that appreciated Lynn's radiance. Rather than being threatened, she recognized that her attraction to what Lynn had been projecting that night at the party expressed that she wanted some of that radiance herself.

Lynn showed understanding toward Amy's negative self-image and she was only too happy to help. From experience, she knew how hard it is to emerge from such phases. Lynn suggested they go shopping together, sort through Amy's closets, go for a facial, or to a new hairdresser. On one of their shopping expeditions, Lynn took the opportunity to say how lovely Rosa was and how sad she was not to have a family of her own. Most of the time she was distracted from such thoughts, especially when she was involved in a new love affair, but Ron was not the kind of man she wanted to have a baby with and when she spent time with Amy, she despaired of ever having such joy. Talking about their longings for what the other had prevented their feelings from becoming mired in envy, or worse in self-disgust. Amy didn't deny Lynn's pain and upset. She responded in a way that allowed Lynn to cry and talk about her fear that she might never find a man she wanted to be with. Lynn felt better because she didn't always have to cover up her negative feelings about being single or her longings for a family.

Such conversations didn't eliminate the pain for either one of them, but it moved the focus from envy and self-hatred to Lynn and Amy's own desires. Coping with those desires is possible once the upset that has been projected onto someone else (with its inevitable distortions) is returned to its real source. Lynn's sexiness and Amy's family life were attributes each desired. Instead of berating themselves for these desires, they began to help one another accept them and try to fulfill them.

As we pointed out in chapter 3, almost all women unconsciously transfer a version of the hopes and restrictions of their own mother-daughter relationship to their current relationships. Women relating to each other see not just their friends or colleagues, they project onto them a whole range of emotions that reflect the legacy of their relationships with their mothers. They want support for autonomous development, but they expect disapproval. They want permission for their sexuality, but they fear punishment. They want to be cared for, but they fear they will be judged for having needs. Untangling the projections and the fantasies that fuel such feelings is part of our current psychological struggle. One woman's success is often threatening to another. But why? The answer has been clearly expressed by hundreds of women we have worked with. They describe feeling deserted, left, abandoned as the other woman moves on and develops. It feels as though the successful one is turning her back, leaving her friend to stay stuck in the space they once shared. At the same time the woman who is a success feels alone in the new and unknown space. She may feel guilty about her achievements. Fearing that she is deserting the lot of women (her friend, her mother, her sister) she discounts what she has. She attempts to minimize it, to deny and hide her achievement. These dynamics, through which a woman feels guilty for her success while other women feel envy, were at work in a group of women psychologists in Chicago.

Hilary's work on child abuse was considered timely by the media and was given special attention. The Psychology Research Center where she worked was catapulted to national recognition. Hilary was asked to give interviews and speak on the topic all around the country. She became an accessible and visible authority and was able to make important statements about the nature of the problem and the treatment options that existed for victims and perpetrators.

Hilary was extremely pleased with the opportunity to do this work and to attract such positive publicity for the center, but she found the exposure personally difficult (who, me?). The tightly knit group of six who constituted the center's professional staff began to seem like a group of five from which she was somewhat excluded. She couldn't put her finger on anything explicit but it *felt* to her as though she was now disliked and that her colleagues were critical of her. She began to feel uncomfortable around them and was aware of a great deal of tension.

During this time it was her husband, rather than her colleagues, who became her main support. He was impressed with her work and pleased for her that she was

being given the opportunity to have it widely understood.

When Hilary had first been asked to comment on
child abuse she had been extremely nervous. The staff
had rallied around her, coaching her, trying to alleviate
her anxiety, and promising to stand by her. Now that she
was clearly capable of doing such things, they found it
hard to know how to relate to her. They had known how
to support her in her weakness but they were uncertain
about how to support her in her strength. To them, by
becoming a spokesperson and managing that on her
own, she had crossed a threshold. She didn't appear to
need them in the same way any more. She had shown
herself to be capable and confident and separate, which
they all envied and feared. No one knew how to remain
connected on this new basis and so they disconnected. In
so doing, they cut off her anchor.

In disentangling the threads, Hilary could see that
she had indeed contributed to her own isolation and the
problems at the center. She had not been able to admit
how much pleasure she was getting from the public recognition. She was not able to share with her colleagues
how her confidence had grown. She empathized with
their nervousness toward the media and the public, but
no longer felt exactly as they did. She found herself
hiding her growth. She could not distinguish between
telling a friend about some of the good things that were
currently happening and feeling she was boasting.
There was no way for her to share her good fortune
without feeling that she was provoking envy.

Hilary's colleagues were, in fact, feeling uncomfortable about several things. On the one hand, they resented

their center being solely identified with her work on child abuse to the exclusion of other research interests. On the other hand, they were scared and envious of her growing stature and self-confidence. It was something they individually aspired to but couldn't imagine achieving.

They were unable to examine their own envious feelings toward the success of their colleague. They found them disagreeable and predictably they had transformed them into something else—either private self-doubt and inadequacy or rejection and anger toward Hilary. The tension increased to such a pitch that accusations began to fly that she was competitive, self-serving, and taking advantage of them. They felt they had all supported her and that once she made it, she no longer needed them.

This change in what was once a mutually supportive relationship, points to the difficulties all of the women at the center had in Hilary's development toward separateness and autonomy. Any of them might have had Hilary's experience had another specialty been picked up by the media. The people experiencing the various feelings would have been different, but the themes most likely would have been the same.

So much of women's relating revolves around supporting one another through difficult times. When a woman seems to be doing well, however, support may be less forthcoming and she may feel that she has been cast out of the company of women. Hilary herself had no desire to reject her colleagues or their intellectual and emotional companionship. She was as much in need of it as ever. She had begun to trust that her professional knowledge was sound, but she was still on fairly shaky ground emotionally and criticism or rejection from her colleagues stoked up her *own* conflicts about ambition. *She felt guilty about her growth* and isolated.

The ambition to be seen and heard as a distinct individual, combined with wanting to be part of a group; to want to feel confident and not hide one's strengths, coupled with an inability to feel that such desires are legitimate—these conflicts are the mainspring of the problems entangling Hilary and her colleagues. Once Hilary was in the limelight, it raised the other women's own desires for recognition—desires that they had not believed were within their grasp and that hence had not been conscious. They envied her apparent ability to take the challenge in her stride and instead of being proud and positive about their colleague, they felt inadequate, depressed, and resentful. Her success brought them in contact with their own ambitions and longings: longings for recognition, for self-confidence, for the independent identity that is still so new for women today. And yet, their own psychological barriers remained. *Tragically, as they held themselves back they unconsciously felt driven to hold back another woman.* Her success, both public and private, symbolized differentiation and her differentiation stirred up too many conflictual feelings. It broke the known and binding merged attachment that had prevailed at the center.

The situation began to improve when Brenda, another researcher at the center, and Hilary initiated an honest talk about what was happening. As we shall see in chapter 8, the impasse was broken by conversations that were direct and honest.

Behind the feeling of envy lies not the spoiling, ungenerous destroying person that is so much the woman's experience of herself when she is gripped by envy. What we find rather is a person so deeply conflicted about her own wants and desires, that she is frightened by others' capacity to respond to theirs. She admires the others but can't understand how they can pursue what she feels so unable to pursue. She envies their capacity to give to themselves in a way that feels deeply forbidden to her. She is stunned by others' capacity to self-actualize. We are in awe of her. We may want to do that ourselves, but cannot imagine how we could. When we see another woman groping toward self-development, unconsciously we may be so threatened that we try to discourage her. *In other words, what envy tells us about is the extent to which women feel unentitled, and undeserving. It is not so much that women are envious. Envy immobilizes us and pinpoints our much deeper conflict about wanting.*

The emergence of envy can be seen in this light as a signpost to desire; a psychological defense, if you like, against women's wanting. It is not something to be suppressed as unsisterly but an emotional response that we need to pay attention to. Defenses develop to ward off, protect, conceal, and distract inner needs that the developing person fears cannot be met.

The defense of envy allows one to project the feelings out where they are experienced as less internally disruptive and challenging. A partial solution is the idea that if only a woman had what she envies, she would be all right. But paradoxically, such ideas feed feelings of powerlessness and leave the woman believing that her hands are tied. Rather than allowing an active state of self-nurturance and development, she feels helpless, passive, needing to be rescued by an outside source.

Thus, envy shows us the craving, the strength of

desire caught up in self-repression, which is projected onto others. It is not a sign of unsisterliness, but a psychological reflection of the current conditions of femininity. We can understand other women's envy as a sign that they haven't given up; they still want. We can help one another with these desires, rather than stifle the feelings of envy as though they were indeed poisonous and spoiling. In coming to grips with what is behind the envy, we create an opening in the merged attachment.

Envy is a contentious concept within psychoanalytic theory. Freud is well-known for his early work on the concept of female penis envy and his finding that girls must overcome their envy (by converting it into the desire to reproduce) and accept their lack of a penis on their way to achieving womanhood. There has been many a caricature of a Freudian analyst wagging his finger over a female insisting that she accept her inadequate biological and social status.

Melanie Klein, an influential figure in modern psychoanalysis, saw envy as a feature of normal development. For Klein, envy occurs first in relation to the mother's breasts or the bottle. However adequate the mother is, Klein argues, the baby cannot control this real and symbolic source of goodness. The baby envies the mother's capacities, wants them for her own, and wishes to deprive the mother of the richness that is in the "feeding breast." For Klein, each child comes into the world with a genetic endowment of envy (and aggression) that is softened or exacerbated by environmental circumstances, such as the mother's capacity or difficulties in tolerating the baby's aggression. If these negative spoiling feelings in the baby can be tolerated by the mother, then the baby can pass through this phase to the next one, in which the capacity for remorse and gratitude for what is given can be expressed.

Although these views may seem radically different, they are really quite similar. In the original Freudian view, it is the representative of the masculine that is envied, while in the Kleinian view it is the mother's breast and the feminine that is envied. Yet, both Klein and Freud believe that envy is primary in itself and has to be faced as such. There is an inevitability, a constitutional makeup, to the occurrence and persistence of envious feelings.

From our point of view, however, Freud's and Klein's observations bear reinterpreting. For the feeling of envy (while it can be extremely powerful in itself and can lead to destructive and spoiling impulses) can be better understood in relation to a child's struggles out of the early stages of dependency and merged attachments toward separation and selfhood. As we've seen, because of the merged attachment in the mother-daughter relationship, separation is especially problematic. The child who recognizes that it does not live within mother's boundaries, that mother is not an extension of it, can feel frightened. Even though a mother's subjectivity may well be fused with that of her child, the mother's actions are not necessarily in tune with or controllable by the child. At various moments the child is forced to recognize mother's independence. The child may make many efforts to deny this, to control mother. And much frustration and rage is expressed when this effort fails. Both penis envy and envy of the breast can be understood as desires for what the child perceives the parent has (apparent self-containment and personal power). Envy is a question about having sufficient supplies oneself: "Do I have enough of what you have inside of me?" "Am I safe enough to be my own person?"

Simple examples of envy occur all the time and entail the same dynamics as the more convulsed and painful instance of Hilary and her colleagues in Chicago. Let's look at two commonplace examples of how envy comes between women and what can be done about it.

When twenty-eight-year-old Joyce tells her friend Rose that she has a new job as a senior buyer in the fashion department of Bloomingdale's, Rose, who is twenty-nine and apparently not ambitious, feels a twinge of envy. She remembers conversations they had had in college when Joyce vowed not to settle for less than she thought she was worth. Rose had always marveled at Joyce's aspirations. When they had worked in the same office, she had felt Joyce's support and the two of them had been promoted together. Joyce had already received several promotions and bonuses since she moved into retail two years ago. Rose doesn't want Joyce's actual job, but she wants the self-confidence and the status, power, and recognition Joyce enjoys. Rose works in middle management for a wine producer and would like a promotion, but she can't imagine being rewarded in this way. She doesn't feel deserving. She denies her own ambition to herself, but envies Joyce her promotion.

Jane and Monika are best friends. They met when they were both just out of college and working as very junior assistants in a publishing house. They were both energetic, thoughtful, and likable and in their early thirties had become senior editors for different publishing companies. Monika had a baby first and came back to work exhausted but exhilarated, just as Jane was about to have her baby. The two women had lots in common: their work, their babies, their outlook on life. When Jane's baby was about ten months old, some of her energy returned, but between baby, home life, reading and editing manuscripts, and keeping the other aspects of her job going, she had little time for herself. She felt dissatisfied with the way she looked and the way she felt in her body. Monika, meanwhile, had acquired a whole new wardrobe and was trimmer and fitter than before her pregnancy. Jane felt envious. She couldn't imagine how Monika managed to find time for herself. When Monika turned down lunch one day in favor of her exercise class, Jane felt mortified—a reaction far stronger than she might have thought appropriate to a simple refusal of a lunch date. Jane's envy wouldn't dissipate. She raged inside about Monika's selfishness and then felt bad about envying her best friend. In talking to her husband about how angry she was with Monika, she realized that she wanted to make more of an effort to be selfish, in the way that Monika was selfish. She realized that she wanted to make more of an effort on her own behalf. In other words, she was able to use the discomfort of her envy to remind herself that she wanted some new clothes. She was still dressing sloppily because her baby dribbled and could ruin new things, but in fact Jane wanted more expressive clothes. She was not happy dressing with the baby in mind all the time. By accepting her own wanting (and in this case since the wanting was reasonably easy to satisfy), she was able to enjoy rather than envy Monika's new outfits.

In the first example, Rose cannot conceive of going after what she wants. She lacks self-confidence, and pursuing her desires is outside her experience and her expectations. Not that she isn't ambitious—she is. But this ambition is painful to her and seems out of reach. Her ambition is denied and her psychic energy is diverted to envying Joyce. Her envy, in effect, keeps her where she is and prevents her from exploring her own ambition and the difficulties that surround it. Envy expresses her inner feelings of unentitlement to advance or pursue her ambition, but she need not remain in this state. In the second example, we have seen that once Jane understood her envy as a signpost to her *own wanting,* she could get behind the initial discomfort that it engendered. When we contact our desire, we can choose to act on it or not. We can grapple directly with the impediments, be they practical issues like a baby that dribbles, or with the conflicts that the wanting stirs up. We can try to come to grips with the internal voices that sabotage the pursuing of our desires.

For Rose and many women, the situations which lead to their envy cannot be resolved so simply. As we have seen, women have come to identify gratifying their needs with meeting needs in others. Even though this is a far from satisfactory state of affairs, it *is* by and large what women were brought up to expect and many have accustomed themselves to a role and a self-image in which they thrive on being needed. The process of forging new identities and discovering the shortcomings of being so attuned to the needs of others, brings women more awareness of their own needs—needs to initiate, needs for recognition, needs for support, and so on. But women are taking on new identities without a psychological feeling of well-being about putting their own needs on the agenda. They may believe wholeheartedly in women's rights or in personal rights; they may believe they should make the effort to pursue whatever they want, in whatever direction. But beliefs and feelings are not always so confluent. Simply believing that self-expression ought to be allowed to women does not necessarily make it all right. For example, many a woman has found herself sabotaging her own success. This is not conscious and certainly not intentional and yet we have to be able to observe the uncomfortable and distressing phenomena of women who apparently undercut themselves in their careers and in their relationships.

On the face of it, this phenomenon is hard to confront; it sounds like blaming the victim. This is not our intention. We need to understand adequately a situation in which, for example, a young and extremely promising woman has done badly in her oral exam for a Ph.D. in physics. A wish to fail is too simple an explanation. More likely is a fear of the implications of success.

Sandra wants to become a theoretical physicist. Her mother gave up her scientific career when she married and Sandra is determined that that won't happen to her. All through college she worked hard. In graduate school she faced tremendous opposition to her choice of subject. People always assumed she was a technician, or teased her ambitions by calling her Madame Curie. No one was neutral about her presence in the program. She was never treated like the male physicists who were supported, allowed to make the occasional mistake, and accepted for their work. She coped with discrimination, teasing, and a certain level of social ostracism. But one professor was supportive and indicated his faith in her capabilities. So why is she giving up now?

She appears to be crumbling at the moment of success because, as we discovered in her therapy, success would confront her with a feeling that she is accomplished. Inside, she doesn't feel entitled to that accomplishment; she doesn't deserve it. It does not feel real; she feels like a fraud; it is so unfamiliar that in some sense she no longer knows herself. She is more comfortable in the battle itself. She can pursue her desire to be a physicist only when it is fueled by opposition. Her internal conflicts find a perfect expression in the attitudes of those around her and so she can rise above their opposition, even excel in the face of it. But getting her Ph.D. would signify the end of the external opposition. She would then be left to experience directly her own conflicts and the *internal* taboos against her own ambition and belief in herself.

It became the task of the therapy to help her struggle through to the acknowledgment of her own wanting and the working through of the internalized taboos against getting. Accepting her success signified psychological separation and this was tremendously frightening for her. Although she had been determined not to repeat her mother's life, she felt a certain guilt as she crossed the threshold that would ensure that she could stay in science. She knew it was what she wanted but a part of her felt uneasy. She was in unexplored and unknown territory. She was psychologically unaccustomed to the notion that she would be allowed to have what she wanted. Moving from a position of unentitlement, of continual anger about not getting, to a position of achieving and succeeding is an enormous psychological shift. It involves the transition from one kind of sense of self to another. In the process, there well may be confusing feelings of depersonalization and loss.

For some women, the wanting that is behind the envy is unbearable. Sally felt envious toward Joy because of Joy's good marriage. Sally's husband had left her suddenly. Her ability to trust men had been severely damaged and Sally was forever warning Joy that she shouldn't rely so fully on her husband. Every time Joy told her about a fight, disappointment, or disturbance in her marriage (no matter how minor or commonplace), Sally leaped at the opportunity to remind her friend that she shouldn't expect more, that this is the way men are. Being the bearer of bad fortune and predictions was an expression of Sally's envy for Joy's situation. She wanted to pierce Joy's idyllic picture, for the pleasure Joy was experiencing was very painful to witness. Beyond her envy, of course, lay her wanting a warm and trusting relationship. She missed the closeness she had once had with her husband and she despaired of finding another man, especially now that she had a child. She would rage about the situation from time to time and feel frustrated, alone, and terribly stuck. The collapse of her marriage seemed to confirm for her the futility of the whole endeavor—her attempt at a close relationship with a man. Spoiling or wishing to spoil Joy's pleasure was an attempt to deny what Joy had and in so doing suppress her own wanting.

Envy then is a catalyst for an exploration of other feelings. Sally's envy was a defense, against feelings which she found even *harder* to cope with. Sally's task is to approach the envy as a shield that can now be removed to reveal the deeper personal issues. It is not simply envy in itself that Sally has to come to terms with—which, of course, she does need to be able to do—but rather she needs to face her pain and the longing she has for an intimate relationship. One day, Joy became really annoyed with her for always latching onto any difficulties Joy had with Mike. Joy's rebuke brought Sally up short. She realized that spoiling—in her mind—what Joy had, didn't do what it was designed to do. It didn't remove Sally's pain, her longing, her feelings of unentitlement. It only made Sally feel temporarily relieved of her own despair. In her disbelief and uncertainty that she can have what she wants, she wished to do away with her friend's contentment. She feels that she can only bear her pain if no one else has what she wants.

This is a common phenomenon. The prohibitions against wanting are so strong in women that it is very difficult to feel genuine joy about something a friend has that we ourselves desperately want. Joy's anger helped to change a bad dynamic. Sally took it as an opportunity to think about why she was being so mean. The more Sally could accept her current pain, the less she translated that pain and upset into the spoiling feelings associated with envy. She became more in touch with her feelings of wanting, and agonizing as they were, they did not threaten her friendship or lead her to undermine her friend's pleasure.

A similar and nowadays extremely common situation took place in Linda and Joan's friendship. When Linda became pregnant at thirty-eight, Joan, who was herself forty and ambivalent about having children, tried to be enthusiastic for Linda's sake, but her feelings got in the way. Although when they spoke on the telephone or went out together, they talked a lot about their mutual work interest in film, Joan found herself dreading the time when the conversation would turn to babies and

Linda's pregnancy. At those moments she felt so envious that it was all she could do to stay in her seat. Hearing about the birth plans, or how Linda's breasts ached, or how much food Linda was eating, or how Mark and Linda were going to spend a last romantic holiday for the two of them, almost made her retch. She was literally sick with envy and could hardly concentrate on the conversation.

What perplexed Joan so was that she wasn't aware of definitely wanting a baby herself. The truth was almost the opposite and that made her uneasy. She had been in a stable relationship for several years and whenever the issue of whether to start a family came up, she realized she wasn't sure she wanted to. She liked her work as a film editor very much; it involved a lot of traveling and interesting challenges. She and Jonathan enjoyed their freedom and flexibility and apart from occasionally feeling a kind of existential angst that something was missing, they were quite content without a child. The difficulty for Joan was deep-rooted doubt that it was all right for her not to have a baby, coupled with her fear of having a baby. She didn't think she would be a good mother and she couldn't see herself giving up her own interests and devoting herself to a baby. She was ashamed of these feelings and hated it when her dreams forced them into her consciousness. Sometimes she would wake up in the middle of the night, panic-stricken about being forty and childless. But in her conscious mind, she didn't want a baby and couldn't really see herself with one.

Joan, like so many women today, is part of the first group of women who have had a kind of a choice about becoming mothers. The incredible freedom and added options provided by contraception are against a background wherein Joan, like other women of her generation, grew up believing that she would and should become a mother. The option to do otherwise is a recent overlay, not a possibility presented with equal validity. Consequently, Joan lives with a sense of discomfort strong enough to prevent her from making a decision. She hasn't come to terms with not having a baby and yet she doesn't feel that she wants one.

As Linda's pregnancy proceeded, Joan felt more and more insincere in her reactions, and when the baby finally arrived, although Joan was happy for Linda and relieved that everything went well, she felt nauseous and anxious whenever she visited Linda. She was scared to pick up the baby, worried that she would drop it or that it would start to cry. Whenever she and Jonathan babysat, she felt wretched. Jonathan suggested that perhaps she wanted a baby and that they should start trying, but Joan was alarmed by the idea and became very cross with him whenever he brought it up. When Linda raved about how wonderful motherhood was, adding that Joan should really try it, Joan broke down and sobbed. Out tumbled her upset and distress and the bad feelings she had about herself because she felt she didn't want to and couldn't be a mother.

As she cried with Linda, she was able to tell her that she had envied Linda's ability to know what she wanted. She wished she had Linda's unambivalent desire to have a child. She wished she felt that way, or at least felt clearly and strongly that she didn't want one. The issue of babies was painful to her, but her distress was compounded by her difficulty in making a decision. For years she had been able to push the dilemma away, but her best friend's pregnancy forced her into an emotional whirl-wind of envy, shame, and fear. Talking with Linda dissipated the envy enough that she could see that she needed to confront these issues more squarely and that her envy represented her own longing to resolve this area of her life.

These examples perhaps can put the concept of envy in women in a more understandable context. They underline our assertion that envy is a signpost to wanting and in that light, as uncomfortable as these feelings may be, we can see them as rebellion and resistance to deprivation; attempted declarations of desire; psychological reflections of a competitive and divisive culture that has one believing in a theory of emotional scarcity, i.e., if one has, there isn't enough for the other to have as well.

We can feel guilty for our strivings and seek punishment for them. The unconscious equation that fulfilling oneself, succeeding in one's career, or achieving a personally satisfying love relationship, is a betrayal of another woman (mother) is extremely common. We can imagine or project onto one another disapproval and in this way we hold each other back. We can become threatened when a woman differentiates, when she deserts the image and practice of femininity we have all grown up in. We can become frightened when a woman doesn't act like a victim. We can become both exhilarated and alarmed by a woman who projects internal strength, who refuses to pretend things are worse for her than they are, who seems to have overcome certain difficulties in her socialization process. Women's friendships today undergo the tremendous stress of juggling a variety of difficult factors. On the one hand, women are making tremendous gains in their professional and work lives; on the other hand, as we've seen, these gains produce emotional waves and reactions. Feelings of envy are increasingly familiar to all women. In groups, in organizations, or between friends, these feelings challenge us to support one another, to overcome the envy or the guilt, and to push forward to meet the longings that have up until now been only fantasies. In accepting our longings, we can address them directly and act on them, bearing in mind that there will be conflicts and uncertainties to face in this new and foreign emotional territory.

Chapter 6

Competition

Feelings of competition often go hand in hand with women's feelings of envy. As in all categories of emotional experience that women are reinvestigating and redefining for themselves, the phenomena of competition, the feelings of competition, the concept of competition are problematic. Competition among women has historically centered on getting men's attention. Women have competed with each other to have the prettiest dress, the newest hairdo, the sweetest personality. The energy involved was considered reasonable and understandable in the days when women's lives were inevitably attached to men's. Women saw each other as rivals in a fight for men's attention and were often portrayed in movies and storybook romances as endlessly resourceful in their attempts to beat a competitor.

From today's perspective, realizing the importance of women's relationships, it seems unlikely that the aim of such competition, of making oneself attractive, was simply directed toward getting men's attention. For many women, men provided the excuse or the conscious reason for making an effort with oneself, but the real target, just as often, was for women's attention. Women have always sought each other's approval and competed among themselves to get it.

From childhood on, we have sought approval and recognition from women more than from men. We have wanted our mothers' attention and have had to compete for it against other children, family responsibilities, outside work, or her separate interests. For girls especially, the loss of our mother's attention, which we have all experienced in the inconsistent nature of the mother-daughter relationship, and the encouragement to cope with that loss by caring for others, often leaves girls feeling insecure. They turn to boys and men, which replenishes some of the attention once so badly needed, but this does not replace the care and attention a woman may still yearn for from another woman. Nothing can. Throughout their lives women manage that loss in a variety of ways. Sometimes the warm and nurturing contact of very close friendships heal the unarticulated and even unconscious wounds of the past; sometimes women manage the loss by appearing aloof as though they do not need; sometimes they choose girlfriends who let them down, thus reconfirming the original injury they experienced with their mothers' turning away. For most women, a variety of responses operate at the same time so that while a woman may have close friends with whom she is not rivalrous or actively competitive, a part of her may still be insecure with them. She wants to please them, in part because she likes them, and in part to ensure that she can hold their attention.

That is not to deny that women are not rivals for

men's attention. Of course they are and have been. In the past a woman's social position, her visibility, even her name (Mrs. . . .) largely depended on the status of a man—first that of her father and later that of her husband. Thus, the competition to get the right man was a serious business and its results shaped many features of a woman's day-to-day existence. But the effort to compete, and the precipitant distrust of other women was relieved by women's friendships. In a sense, friendship was the best defense against rivalry, for a woman could feel reasonably sure that her friend would not compete with her for a man. Of course occasionally women let each other down and broke the pact of friendship.

Joleen's best friend "stole" her boyfriend and her job, leaving Joleen in a state of shock, friendless, loverless, and unemployed. Joleen and Caroline had met in Brussels where they were both working in public relations for American corporations. They had gravitated toward one another because they were both in their thirties, single, career-minded, and enjoyed going out together. Together they would try to meet men and Joleen was very happy when she met Simon, an Englishman working in Brussels for the European Economic Community. Now they were often a threesome, or a foursome if Caroline brought along a date. Joleen was very happy. She had everything she wanted. Caroline meanwhile was dissatisfied with the career prospects at her company and Joleen arranged for her to see her boss as that department was expanding. They fantasized about how much fun it would be for them to work together.

When Joleen returned from a two-week business trip to Chicago, her boss told her that he was so impressed with Caroline that he had hired her to oversee the expansion. Joleen was furious. She'd never expected such an outcome, nor was she prepared for the affair between Simon and Caroline that had started while she was away. Although they both felt guilty, Simon and Caroline had convinced themselves that Joleen would be able to accept this development and that their threesome would now include a sexual triangle. Joleen was incredibly distraught. She saw no reason to accept sharing Simon and did not care to try to find one. She felt she could trust neither of them again. She found it impossible to work in the same office as Caroline and she left her job, although she wasn't immediately able to find another one.

Two years after this string of events Joleen told a workshop on women's relationships how much she still hurt, how she missed her friend, and how angry and murderous she had felt toward Caroline. She couldn't understand how these things had happened, because to her, what was sacred in friendship was the trust that what was important to one would not be derided or snatched away by the other. Almost everyone in the workshop nodded in recognition when Joleen expressed these sentiments, for women count on this bond between them.

As a little girl growing up in the American South in the 1950s, Joleen, like so many other little girls, had taken part in ceremonies, some involving the exchange of blood pricked from little fingers, in which she and a friend pledged mutual fidelity. In those days, fidelity meant keeping other girls out of the friendship or the clique or sharing a particular hatred of a teacher or type of girl. These confidences and the shared dislike of others were the building blocks of friendship as much as the sharing of similar interests, ideas, and dreams. Keeping others out and being able to put them down, was a safe mechanism for a girl's negative feelings (one of the few). But focussing on the dreadful outsider was really a mechanism for creating a safe place for the insiders. The need to feel attached and special to another girl is a longing that dominates other emotions. The competition, which seems so apparent, shields to some extent the more pressing and underlying need for safe, attached, love with a woman.

Competition is endemic to women's relationships in every arena. One moment, girls and women compete about who is the best dressed and in the next moment they compete about who is the worst off in any given situation. "You haven't heard anything yet," says Sue, preparing to tell her divorce settlement story to a new acquaintance. "You think you had it bad, well my ex-husband takes the cake." We swallow our guilt for having been self-indulgent enough to think we were worst off and we listen diligently to the other person's story. We compete about how *well* we are doing and we compete about how *badly* we are doing. The competition disguises something else—a desperate need for attention, for someone to listen and to appreciate how it has been for us. We want the particulars of a given situation to be heard. We want our own private struggles to be authenticated by others and we can't imagine that this will happen without drama. It isn't competition per se that shapes the presentation, it is a fear that one won't be listened to (that one is invisible), that fuels the competition.

Kate is one of three daughters from a middle-class family in Albany.

Kate experiences a tremendous amount of competition with her sisters. She continually feels a strong need to distinguish herself from the others. In their way, her parents encouraged this by praising different attributes in each of them. Linda was the bright one who did well in school; Maggie was the outgoing one with a sparkling personality; and Kate was seen as the beautiful one. But despite the parents' efforts to give each one a special place, family and friends referred to them as "the girls." When, at thirty-two, Kate became the first of her sisters to become pregnant, she gloried in the attention of her parents, her aunts, her uncles, and her friends. Three months later as Kate entered the second trimester of her pregnancy, Maggie announced that she too was pregnant. Kate was beside herself with rage. She felt that Maggie had intentionally and willfully taken something from her. She found it almost impossible to express any happiness for Maggie and dreaded spending any time with the whole family.

For three months, Kate had had what she always longed for—recognition and attention for herself from her parents; for three months she had the experience of departing from being one of the girls; for three months she had felt that she was being seen as uniquely herself, as Kate. Now just three short months later she was filled with the all-too-familiar feelings of competition. Once again, as one of the girls, she felt unrecognized and un-seen as an individual. For Kate, competitive feelings were rooted in her struggle to be seen in her separate identity.

Recent attempts by many women to see other women as allies rather than potential rivals has meant that the feelings of competition may have been tempo-rarily stifled or managed in a slightly different way. But for most women, a dose of political insight or heart-felt sloganeering have not eliminated competition. Actually, the situation today is perhaps even more difficult than it was a generation or two ago.

Today, as women struggle to take their place in the world, to expand their vistas, to undertake the challenge of new things, ready-made masculine ideology is being thrust upon them. It goes roughly like this: The world out there is tough. If you want to make it out there you need to be tough. You need to know how to compete, to be single-minded, and firm. Competing is something men can and have done, it is bred into them, and women who want a slice of the cake are just going to have to be able to take the pressure and compete on male terms. It's no good going all soft and feminine on the job. Competition is the name of the game in a capitalist society. The strong survive and they survive by competing and by being on their toes all the time. In other words, women take note: you should be competing, for competition is a critical element of success.

It is ironic that much of the energy that initially propelled the Women's Liberation Movement gathered strength from a consensus that competition among women is destructive; it divides women and makes them distrust one another. Today, largely as a result of the campaigns organized by the feminist movement, women are now finding that more doors are open to them. But instead of an infusion of feminine sensibilities accompanying women's entry in significant numbers into new kinds of jobs in the work force, we are witnessing instead the applauding of masculine values at the work place and at home. Where once a few lone women in male jobs were seen as aggressive or ballbreaking (i.e., not real women), now women are encouraged to be as aggressive as men on the job. Meanwhile, women who for years were alone in toughing it out in male preserves may have become so accustomed to competing on male terms that they are unsympathetic to the challenge of thinking about work relations in a different way. Masculine values are strengthened as they are enacted by women.[8]

The whole culture applauds and condones competition in one way or another. Competitive ranking is embedded in our social relations. Competition is something even those committed to social change for women applaud. Lillian Rubin in her lovely exposition on friendship advocates that women become more skilled about dealing with their competitive feelings. "It isn't that the women don't have competitive feelings, only that they have much more difficulty in acknowledging them, therefore acting on them. Yet their inhibitions about competition can damage their friendships almost as much as men's facility with it harms theirs. Indeed, it is precisely because women have, for so long, been constrained from expressing their competitive strivings cleanly and clearly that they can become distorted into the kind of petty rivalries, jealousies and envy that sometimes infect their relationships with each other. . . . As a psychotherapist, I believe one of my tasks is to help women to contact their competitive strivings more directly and to express them more openly. . . ."[9]

But this is too simple a prescriptive. In order to understand competition, what it means to women, and why they experience it as they do, we need to address questions similar to those we asked when examining envy. As we shall see, masculine concepts do not serve us well in the analysis of competition among women.

Competition plays a different psychological role in the lives of men and women. Because of this we cannot import an essentially masculine concept without re-thinking it. Just as envy, we argued, is a defense against a complex of other feelings, so too is competition a start-ing point in our understanding. Feelings of competition are disagreeable, but they are not simply an emotional state of affairs that just have to be grappled with (or applauded). Competitive feelings are a signpost to other feelings, a defense structure that, uninvestigated, clouds a relationship with difficult and unworkable tensions.

Let's look briefly at girls' and boys' psychological development to see why the concept of competition has such different meaning for each gender. A crucial devel-opmental task facing girls centers around being able to see oneself as *alike but separate* from one's mother. But, as we have seen, because mothers and daughters share gen-der, and because a mother identifies with her daughter and may not herself have a separated psychology (either from her own mother or her daughter), this developmen-tal task is no easy process and many women are engaged in a lifelong struggle to establish a separate identity for themselves. Boys and men, however, are related to as "other" from the beginning. They are unlike their moth-ers, they do not share their gender, they are fundamen-tally different biologically and they will have a different social existence than their mothers. And so, boys are defined and have been defined in opposition to the femi-nine. They are familiar with otherness and difference because a boundary derived from gender difference affects the shape of the merged attachment in the mother-son relationship. Boys are treated as other and experience themselves as other from early on and so the infant merger and the steps toward differentiation of self follow a different path.[10] Opposition is a stance that *upholds and supports* a masculine identity. Competition spurs the process of differentiation. It is an act of self-hood (albeit a defensive one). *Whereas women search for self through connection with others, men search for self through distinguishing themselves from others.* Thus competition for men is often about calling attention to difference in the service of selfhood. For women, differentiation can feel like a threat to self-identity. It would, therefore, be a mistake to see competition between women as simply an expression of striving and a skill they should be encouraged to adopt or give vent to. We must first come to grips with what women describe as their difficulties with competitive feelings and then explore those with reference to women's psychological history.

For so many women the struggle for a separate identity is almost a psychic impossibility. Competing and differentiating feel equivalent to a severing of connection—a connection which has provided the woman with her sense of self. As we discussed in chapter 3, the concept of differentiating, i.e., the capacity to be separate and still remaining connected within the relationship is outside women's psychological reference points.[11] To recapture the metaphor we used then, it is ungrammatical. It doesn't fit in with a woman's experience of herself or of other women. If one competes, one is in some sense contesting the merged attachment. The woman is saying, "I am not the same, I am different/better/worse." In forcing the separateness or difference to be acknowledged, she stands alone. And once alone or more precisely, unattached, a woman may be left experiencing a shaky self-identity. Thus, competing can be an internally terrifying experience. For in the act of competing, she may feel that she is threatening the relationship with the other. Competition does not hold them together but breaks them apart. She may feel as though she is both annihilating the other woman, while at the same time losing herself.

As a result, many women opt out of competition altogether. It is no wonder women feel bad when they feel competitive. It is no wonder women feel guilty when they feel competitive toward a friend. It is no wonder that competition so alarms us that we often find it painful to admit to or we deny that is what we are really feeling. Presenting oneself as competent can feel too aggressive and self-serving. Finding oneself in a situation in which one has to succeed over other women may be just too uncomfortable because it is seen to sever women's lifeline to other women.

Marion dropped out of the Royal Academy of Dramatic Art (RADA) in London when she was nineteen because, although she was good, very good, she couldn't bear all the vying for attention that she and the other female students were involved with. She just wanted her talents and strengths to be recognized. She didn't want to have to be better than this friend or that one. She found it very threatening and was sure she had made the wrong career choice. She couldn't see herself competing for parts with her contemporaries for the next forty years. She wanted a work situation in which she and others could feel intrinsically valued. Like many women, her need to find a self-identity in relation to others rather than in opposition or competition to them, precluded her from competing. It was simply too uncomfortable. Withdrawing was a more manageable stance for her.

Whenever Claudia, a musician in her mid-twenties, was around Anne and Carol, two of her old friends from high school, who were now both professional dancers, she felt uneasy. With Anne she realized that she would suddenly start feeling diminished. With Carol she felt on edge. Although the topic of conversation usually interested her, she would rarely contribute to it. Whatever she thought about mentioning seemed to revolve around her latest successes and she felt that it would be too pushy on her part to talk about herself. Claudia was an accomplished violinist and wasn't usually shy. She found the time spent with Anne or Carol very disagreeable and tried to understand why she clammed up. What she came to realize was that Anne and Carol were very competitive with her. They would talk about classical music without ever acknowledging her place in that field. They felt so bad about themselves and what they perceived as their lack of success, that they begrudged hers. They tried to make themselves feel better at her expense. By disregarding her special knowledge, they effectively ignored Claudia and who she now was. It was this lack of recognition that raised competitive feelings in her. She felt dismissed and almost banned from taking part in the conversation. It stimulated a strong desire to display her knowledge and force Anne and Carol to acknowledge her, but she was so angry and hurt at being disregarded that she choked up.

Often competition is about the desire for recognition of one kind or another, because outside recognition grants a person visibility. If one feels passed over, unseen, or squashed, feelings of competition may erupt that represent a fight for selfhood. A woman wants her achievements to be noticed, for *her self* to be seen. Claudia wanted to force her presence on Carol and Anne. In being ignored by them, she became invisible. An internal alarm went off, making her fight for her place. Her wanting to talk about her latest accomplishments was about bringing the recognition she had gained elsewhere into a situation in which she wasn't being recognized.

Anne and Carol *were* in fact ignoring Claudia. Their envy stood in the way of their acknowledging her. Because Anne and Carol were each individually conflicted about their own longings, their own ambition, their desire for public recognition, they had to deny what Claudia had achieved. They joined together and excluded her and her contribution. *Their envy stirred up her competitiveness.* Their denial of her made her fight for herself. Let us recall the psychologists in Chicago to illustrate the interplay and differences between envy and competition. We discussed how envious Hilary's colleagues were of her budding self-confidence and her ability to grow into her new public role. But what we did not bring into the story at that time was that, in addition to their envy, they felt competitive. For as well as the repressed ambition that ignited their envy, they had competitive feelings about the recognition she had gained. They wanted an equivalent recognition themselves. They wanted an outside acknowledgment of their competence. Inside, they did not always feel competent and adequate, but they wanted to. If they were in Hilary's shoes, they fantasized, it would mean that they could gain the affirmation she had received, enabling them to feel competent too.

Whereas feelings of envy stem from a taboo against a woman's wanting, feelings of competition stem from the prohibitions women have experienced about their own autonomy and visibility. Unlike envy, the woman feeling competitive is not trapped in conflicted impermissible longings; rather she is struggling with undermining feelings of inadequacy and self-doubt. She doesn't feel capable or competent. She doesn't know how to go about gaining the capability or confidence. She is ashamed to expose her feelings of inadequacy. Admitting this feeling is so humiliating and frightening that it is turned into its opposite: I can do better than you. This element exists even when the competition is over how badly things are going. For if things are very bad, nothing can be done. One is hopeless. Competing about being the best or the worst are two different faces of a defense against facing deep feelings of inadequacy.

In the same way that we can understand aspects of envy as a rebellion against deprivation, so too we can understand the impulses behind competition in a positive light. Women's feelings of competition are an expression of their energy toward life, toward self-actualization, toward differentiation and the right to be one's own person. They are about the desire for separation and selfhood. They are about overcoming crippling feelings of self-doubt and insecurity; they are about wanting to achieve the confidence to fulfill ambition of whatever kind; they are about having and being.

To see them in this new light, however, is not to disregard how painful and humiliating feelings of competition can be. In unraveling the various threads, in investigating the competitive feelings, we are always asking why a woman feels competitive with another woman in a given situation. What is at stake, what is the function of the competitive feeling?

If we reconsider the Southern California dance company that Laurie initiated, we may recall how upset the other members felt when she first went on leave. They had to overcome feelings of abandonment and insecurity. Now that she was about to return to work, they found themselves wary about reintegrating her. Part of their unease was expressed as competition. In understanding what can occur in woman-to-woman competition this example shows us three distinct features: 1) competition for outside recognition (Laurie had recognition as the founder and director), 2) competition as a cover for feelings of inadequacy, and 3) competition in the search to assert a separate identity.

Several of the women revealed that they felt openly competitive with Laurie, her choreographic skills, her ideas, and her flair. During the year she was on leave, without her to rely on, they had been forced to develop talents they didn't know they had. Although they were nervous about doing so, they had performed two new sequences to acclaim. They had gathered for themselves some of the recognition she had previously received and they were loath to give it up.

Because this was a new direction for them as a group and because it followed closely the tremendous insecurity they had felt when she went on leave, her return was threatening. They worried that she would come back and dominate the group. They worried that she would come back and take away what they had accomplished. They worried that she would find their efforts pallid in comparison with her own. They feared that when she returned *they themselves*, not her, would deny the strength they had amassed and that they would be unrecognized by her because they would hide what they were now capable of. Her absence had been long enough to uncover their own feelings of inadequacy, but not quite long enough to consolidate a new source of strength. They were insecure and wanted her approval. At the same time they couldn't imagine they would receive it.

When she had gone on leave, the group inherited a baby (the dance company) it had never parented. They felt very competitive with Laurie in the sense that they wanted to be adequate parents but they feared they were not. They worried that she would see that and feel disappointed in them.

The dilemma of the women involved many of the problems that hide behind the term competitive—feelings of inadequacy, lack of recognition, and a struggle for a new group identity.

Sara and Lesley, both journalists at a local radio station, are forever going on diets together. After three weeks of the latest one, Sara tells Lesley that she has lost twelve pounds. She is terribly pleased with herself and expects Lesley's praise. Lesley instead feels competitive. She's only lost seven pounds and until she heard Sara's news she was feeling quite pleased with herself. Now she feels fat and useless. Sara's triumph doesn't inspire her; it makes her feel panicked. Lesley feels deserted by Sara. They were supposed to be miserable together or successful together. They were meant to be in the same place at the same time. Now Sara has done something to break the bond. All of a sudden there is a competition where there was none before. And in the competition, Lesley is losing. She wishes she could do as well as Sara. She feels competitive. She feels mean for being ungenerous toward Sara.

Lesley's competitive impulses were a simple example of competition functioning as a defense. Her merger with Sara allowed her to feel relatively secure and good about herself. She wasn't alone in her bad feelings about herself and she wasn't alone in seeking (albeit temporary) solutions. When she was doing well on her diet, she was able to feel relatively good in herself. But when Sara told of her success, Lesley instantly experienced herself in relation to Sara. She felt the differences between them. Her good feelings evaporated. Sara's success induced in Lesley a feeling that she would never be good enough, attractive enough, or sufficiently self-disciplined. She felt like abandoning her diet because she was such a failure. These feelings had been kept at bay as long as the agreement to stay in the same place together was in force. When Sara pulled ahead of Lesley, Lesley's competitive feelings made her want to pull ahead too, but her inner experience of inadequacy surfaced simultaneously, stopping her in her tracks.

Of course it wasn't Sara's fault that Lesley felt this way. Lesley's upset was something she had to overcome herself. Sara could help her with it, but she hadn't actually abandoned her by losing more weight. She hadn't been trying to compete with Lesley and do better; she had been trying to do what she wanted for herself. When they talked about how discouraged Lesley felt, Sara tried to renew Lesley's confidence, to help her overcome the feelings of inadequacy that Sara's relative success had engendered.

Is it inevitable for women to feel rivalry toward one another? Is this competition engendered by the mother-daughter relationship? Underlying each competitive situation is there a fear of surpassing what mother has achieved, or perhaps a desire to surpass what mother has achieved?

Of course, themes from the mother-daughter relationship resonate for most women when competitive feelings are evoked. In forging our identities we have had to compete with the overwhelming image of womanhood that mother's presence represents for us. We have needed to reposition ourselves vis-à-vis her. This may be a painful struggle, for finding new options for oneself can feel as though one is rejecting or repudiating a mother's life and what she has given. In order to be a grown-up woman oneself, one may feel that one is betraying or deserting one's mother, getting something mother has never had—the experience of separated selfhood. If mother's identity is derived and maintained from her merged attachments, then a daughter's separation may be resisted. A mother may wish to keep her daughter in the merged attachment in order to maintain her identity.

Mother and daughter may feel that they are engaged in a tug of war. At times, one is pulling for the merged attachment, and the other for differentiation and separateness. Each can find herself on either side of the rope, for they both desire merged attachment and they both desire separation. Neither can win, as long as they go on tugging, because this is not a war, but a joint and separate struggle for selfhood. The daughter, struggling toward adulthood, may therefore feel that each circumstance is full of competition, a test of who will win. Each one feels trapped in the struggle. One feels she has been abandoning and betraying, the other feels she is the prison guard. But this need not be a fight for individual survival based on merger or false separation if both the love, connection, and need they have for each other, as well as the pain and joy of letting go, can be acknowledged.

One obvious area in which we can see the mother–daughter competition emerge is a daughter's developing sexuality. A teenage daughter symbolizes a mother's transition to a different stage of her life. And because our culture places a premium on youthful appearance and sexuality, it is not an unproblematic transition. Sexuality is an asset a woman takes into the world[12]. It is through her sexuality that she is recognized, albeit only partially. Because of this a mother may be fearing her own aging process at the same time that she is encountering, on a daily basis, her daughter's entry into the world of sexuality and womanhood. Her daughter's nubility reminds her of how her physicality was once an important vehicle for her in receiving recognition. Thus, without even being aware of it, a mother may struggle to maintain her self, by sexually competing with a daughter.

Many women have spoken about the ways in which they have felt their mothers became overly intrusive and involved with their boyfriends. Indeed, this is such an accepted part of the culture that it was mythologized in the role Anne Bancroft played as Mrs. Robinson in *The Graduate*. Mrs. Robinson's power, such as it was, was essentially sexual. Her terror of aging, of not being seen as a sexually desirable person, made the emerging sexuality of her daughter too painful. She desperately clung to her own sexual identity as she fought with her daughter for the limelight.

In the various struggles with competitive feelings that women are having to face, we can see a common thread, a common desire that can help us to rehabilitate the notion of competition rather than simply recoil from competitive situations. Instead of feeling terror when we experience competitive feelings, instead of being paralyzed when we feel competitive toward a friend, instead of judging ourselves negatively, we can look at competition as a way of understanding more about ourselves and other women. We can see that it is, in part, a search for recognition, a part of the struggle to self-actualize, to separate psychologically and to be seen as a separate individuated person. It is not about beating the other person out, it is not about being the best, it is not about external accolades per se, it is about using the example of someone else's achievement, in whatever direction, to try to fulfill a personal ambition.

Women's appreciation of other women's successes and achievements can pose problems if we rely on patriarchal definitions to evaluate what is admirable and worth appreciating. In our society, another's achievement is often experienced with competitive feelings. Such responses are deeply embedded in our culture but, we argue, they are internalizations of an order that promotes individualism, self-promotion, and fear of intimate social connection.

Individualism is a reward system and a way of being that fosters false independence. It doesn't require the person to have a secure sense of self. One denies one's dependency on others and continually builds a set of defenses that isolates one from intimate connection with others. Others' achievements can be experienced as a threat, for one relies on a sense of self from outside of oneself. That is, lacking an internally secure sense of self, one builds a personality based on outward achievements.

One is continually thrown back on competitive feelings, for one's very existence rests on external appearance and successes. Tragically, our culture endorses and thrives on this latter formulation. The system we know of competition, dog eat dog, superstar and underdog, is built on individualism.

In contrast, psychological separateness, that is, the ability to feel a sense of oneself and a boundary between self and other, is not the same thing as individualism. Psychological separateness encourages and makes possible fulfilling and authentic connections between people. The ability to achieve a sense of oneself as separate derives from being in a connected relationship and acknowledging one's need for love, interdependency, and emotional connection. This need extends throughout life. Relying on others is a central part of psychological separateness. In building an alternative to destructive competitiveness, we need to pose a different structure to relationships: a structure that can encompass both connection and separateness and the creativity that flows from that tension.

Chapter 7

Anger

Anger is an emotional state that tends to present enormous difficulties for women. We have grown up with two entirely contradictory images about women and anger. On the one hand is the contented, mother figure who accommodates others and for whom nothing is too much. She is unflappable, absorbs everyone else's pain and upset, and projects warmth and ease. Anger and angry feelings never surface in her. On the other hand is the angry, nagging shrew. She is dissatisfied with her lot and flies into a rage at the slightest provocation. It is disagreeable to be around her and her anger is portrayed as vicious and damaging.

These two caricatures of women deny anger a place in their emotional vocabulary. The message we are left with is clear. She is not supposed to feel it, and if she does, she is certainly not supposed to show it. As with their sexuality, women are represented in two extreme ways, saints or shrews (madonnas or whores), and as with their sexuality almost everyone—including the woman herself—is afraid of a woman's anger. In women's relationships with one another, anger is rarely acknowledged or expressed. Although difficulties, disagreements, and inconsiderateness that engender anger are every bit as much a part of friendship as they are part of other intimate relationships, women have no direct outlet for the anger such upsets may cause. Although mothers and daughters may fight with one another, and sisters may squabble incessantly, woman-to-woman relationships outside the family rarely include arguments about personal difficulties, and when a dispute does reach a breaking point, often its tenor is loaded with guilt and accusations, making it intolerable for both parties concerned. Often a rage ensues that terrifies both women, discouraging them from showing their angry feelings toward one another again.

From the introduction to this book you may recall that it was the ferocious anger women expressed in the Women's Studies Program at Richmond College in 1972–73 that had led us into a deeper study of women's psychology and a desire to understand why women who could unite in the face of opposition became immediately adversarial when the external opposition faded into the background. In analyzing now—on a psychological level—what took place in that Women's Studies Program, it is possible to see that the disputes and difficulties which occurred, the political disagreements and differences of opinion that emerged, assumed a psychological significance well beyond the scope of the original strictly political nature of the dispute. In a sense it was as though this dispute, and others similar to it, carried the weight of all the unexpressed difficulties and angers that do exist between women. When these difficulties erupt we are not witnessing a simple difference of opinion but the expression of a very deep emnity that can be stirred up in women. When the love and trust that women count on from each other is eroded, the upset, betrayal, hatred, and rage that is evident is extremely powerful.

At one level, we could say that what happened in the Women's Studies Program, what fueled the anger and feelings of betrayal, guilt, and rage, was a breaking of the merged attachment that had initially held the women in the program together. The members of the department had joined together and created a feeling of security by focusing on their commonality of experience vis-à-vis an outside enemy. The difficulties and differences between women, which women are so unused to dealing with straightforwardly, could be subsumed as long as a forceful outside opposition existed. The opposition strengthened the resolve of the insiders, bound them together, and was a useful dumping ground for the difficulties among the group, which were projected out. When the program had received that little bit of support that allowed it to function, then the disagreements about its philosophy and direction emerged. But these differences were threatening because they represented a challenge to the safety and surety of an attachment based on merger and sameness.

What made the situation so explosive and ultimately so damaging was the way in which certain women could not tolerate difference. They could not hold onto the good feelings in the group and trust that their opinions would be valued unless the whole group agreed with them. These women looked to the group—as a kind of transferential mother figure—to give them the approval, love, and support that they still craved. In other words, the insecurity we have seen that leads friends to want one another to agree with them absolutely or be in exactly the same place at the same time (Lesley and Sara) was exacerbated in this group situation. Their strongly held political position was felt by them to be invalidated—and by extension they were invalidated—unless they could control or dominate the situation. Any diversity of positions was intolerable for it could not sufficiently answer the psychological insecurity of the women who were bonding together in a political arena in order to find psychological security. It was as though unless their position were the dominant or the only position, their *very selves* were in question. The search for identity and selfhood had devolved upon the group and when the group refused to provide that kind of shoring up, the rage that was unleashed was tremendous and destructive.

At the same time, because they were insecure, not used to being taken seriously, listened to, appreciated, and so on, they found it hard to believe that diversity of opinion was valued and that their opinion would carry weight even if not everyone agreed. A woman-only environment had opened up the longing for just that kind of attentiveness. But along with the longing, conscious and unconscious, was the remembrance (conscious and unconscious) that a woman (mother and now the group) could not easily accept separateness and difference.

Psychologically, the group turned from being experienced as a good and nurturing mother, who is enabling and helps one grow through the merged attachment, into a disabling, venomous, withholding, mean traitor that must be destroyed. The group (the mother) could not psychologically provide for all the needs that were unconsciously being brought to it. Nor could it make up for what had been missing in each individual woman's past, in spite of the strong unconscious wish that it could do so. When that unconscious fantasy broke down, the rupture was full of the rage of disappointment and the self-hatred of having believed that such a fantasy might have come true. Disappointment and humiliation arose from having allowed oneself to hope that the program might mend the hurt and anguish left over from the primary mother-daughter relationship. The separateness which the differences revealed was so intolerable that the original unity was repudiated and a premature separation instituted.

The inability to cope with difference that is at the heart of many of women's difficulties with one another is a propelling force in women's anger. Anger plays a role in both the denial of differences and in the assertion of difference. In the Women's Studies Program, the anger served to eliminate a difference that couldn't be handled. The protagonists were caught up in a struggle in which anger and rage became the mechanism for silencing others and asserting oneself. In this sense, it had both destructive and constructive meaning. This happens in other situations too. Often, a woman will feel herself becoming angry when her experience or perceptions are being denied. With the denial it is as though *she, her self* has disappeared. Her anger emerges as an act of self-proclamation. She is asserting her right to be seen, contesting a view that says differences are untenable. And yet this self-assertion may be felt to be problematic because it threatens her links with other women with whom the need for attachment remains.

If we think back to the situation in chapter 6 between

the violinist Claudia and her friends Carol and Anne, we may recall that Claudia felt angry and competitive when she was shut out of the conversation. Her anger at being ignored produced two distinct responses: one response was to clam up, further distancing herself from the conversation; the other was to respond by boasting, trying to force her presence on them. Thus, the anger she felt, which stimulated both responses, contained both negative and positive aspects. On the one hand, it was an alarm bell signaling a fight for visibility in a situation where she was being denied recognition; on the other hand, it further immobilized her, making it extremely hard for her to contribute to the conversation in a way that felt comfortable.

For many women, anger is just like it was for Claudia. It is a signal that all is not all right, but at the same time the person doesn't quite know what to do with it. It may take her over, she may feel shaky, depressed, weepy, or out of control. She may misinterpret her angry feelings and not know what to do with them. Anger is so fundamentally out of place with the cultural stereotype of femininity that even though we have all felt it, observed it, and been the recipient of someone else's anger, we can be scared of it in ourselves.

Much of what is embedded in women's anger is caused by a psychological misreading of a situation. As we have seen, the transferences between women in which they are seen as one another's mothers can sometimes cause confusion in what they are needing, wanting, and anticipating from each other. Often, a woman will project onto a friend disapproval where it doesn't exist, reading in her facial expression or responses the condemnation of her mother. In turn, she feels angry that she has been rejected. She feels she is not allowed to have whatever it is she wants and the anger is a way to bolster her sense of self. In expressing herself or in hearing her anger, she feels stronger.

But, of course, not all angry feelings in women are rooted in the tangle of projections we have referred to. Women feel or become angry when an injustice has occurred, when they have been hurt, when they feel taken advantage of, when they feel misunderstood. The difficulty is that they are often more than reluctant to show this anger to the friend who may have caused it. Similarly, the knowledge that someone is angry with her may make her nervous and fearful. *It is at this point,* not in the recognition of the anger, but *in the anticipated delivery or receiving of it* that the transference projections occur. That is to say, when we were little and we aroused our mother's or father's anger, we felt afraid. The anger they directed at us felt like a withdrawal of love. In that moment, the world became a frightening place, for without the protection and love of a parent, we feel vulnerable and scared. Even if our parents were not all that we would have wished them to be, their withdrawal, synonymous with anger in many families, was a withdrawal we could ill afford, for we still needed them.

By the same token, when we were little and we felt anger in ourselves, we were also frightened. How dare we feel angry at those we still needed so much? To feel anger and especially to express it would be to jeopardize the relationship. We would be cutting ourselves off from the source of comfort and succor. It is easy to observe how anger is related to the development of an individual self. Observing two-year-olds, one can see that it is not that they are terrible, as in the cultural adage, but that they are in the process of differentiating, expressing their differences, asserting their will. When someone else misunderstands what they want, they assert themselves with vigor. The act of assertion, if recognized by the adults, allows them to feel safe in their identity and desires; their anger is understood and tolerated. If the act is continually thwarted, they will rage to preserve a sense of self. The tantrum that follows is an assertion of self, an attempt to protect and insist on their still fragile and developing separate identity.

Another aspect of anger occurs for those women who grew up in families in which angry feelings were forever being expressed, and where violence was part of the family's way of relating. In such cases, anger becomes associated with the capacity to arouse strong feelings. It is a known form of contact. It shows that the other person cares. Although not a version of love, it is an expression of the intensity of feeling. It may signify love to one who has not felt the nurturing, supportive love of a mother or father. Rousing someone to rage, engaging him or her in anger, gives some feeling of power even if it is only a negative power. At the same time, in the combat there is contact and a common experience—albeit a very painful contact.

With this background, anger between women is a volatile area. It touches on the anger of early childhood and threatens the established relationship. But it is not the whole story, for if the anger can be addressed without the person feeling she is out of control or damaging the other, it can be useful to both friends. To express one's anger is to hear oneself, to defend oneself when one has felt invaded, negated, or denied. If Claudia could have expressed her anger directly to Anne and Carol, "I feel angry with the two of you, I don't like being ignored. I want to be included and recognized," she would have found a more authentic expression of her feelings than the boasting that caused her such discomfort. In that act of assertion she would be saying: "See, I have a self. I'm human, I hurt, I want. I am not just a trash can into which you deposit your difficulties." Carol and Anne would, in turn, have had to deal with real criticism and cope with the hurt they were causing. This might have helped them understand why they were so competitive and jealous of her, and how that jealousy hindered their own self-development. It might have been a difficult exchange. One woman confronting two others with her anger about their actions is not an easy task, and yet the relationship had become untenable. The three were bound together in a destructive pattern and Claudia's anger was the signal that the situation was far from all right.

Expressing anger is one side of the difficulty, receiving it another. Many women are intensely self-critical and imagine, in a difficult situation, that they are in the wrong or have not performed up to par.

By accepting criticism from the outside and allowing oneself to think carefully about it, a woman can learn something about herself that will be far more useful than the fantasied guilt and self-blame she may feel. Freida and Melinda were close friends and neighbors in their late twenties who had been in the process of drifting apart over the last few months. Melinda was very angry with Freida because she felt that Freida had withdrawn from her. Freida, meanwhile, had been feeling guilty because she no longer accommodated Melinda in the ways she used to. She wasn't always available when

Melinda called, she didn't help her out with babysitting as much anymore, she wasn't a constant source of emotional replenishment for Melinda.

When Melinda said she felt angry with Freida, it gave Freida a chance to think about why she had been withdrawing. She realized that for a long time she had felt burdened by being such a good giver. Melinda's anger and complaints made her realize that she must have started to rebel against that role, attempting friendship with Melinda and others more on the basis of her own needs than theirs. But because this had been a largely unconscious shift, one she was barely aware of in herself, she wasn't able to tell anybody else about the changes she was going through. Melinda still felt angry and rejected; the explanation didn't soften the hurt. She couldn't help but feel that it was something in *her* that had turned Freida off. But it wasn't, and Freida had to insist and clarify for herself that she had been a compulsive giver, almost addicted to looking out for and after others, and that her withdrawal although it made her feel guilty and anxious, was an attempt to change the basis of her giving. She couldn't commiserate when she didn't genuinely feel like it; she couldn't any longer bury her own needs by taking care of friends' needs. She had her own experience and that had to be recognized. As we shall see in the next chapter, this recognition was expressed in the most minor of ways, but these had deep significance for Freida.

In these last four chapters we have stressed the importance of women recognizing what is troubling them in their relationships with one another. We have illustrated how in even the most minor of ways, confronting these difficulties can be exhilarating. It can encourage the relationship to grow. Much of the guilt, the fear and distrust, the deep disappointments between women, which lead to negative feelings, can be managed when women talk to one another about their experience of one another's actions.

Articulating difficulties, taking responsibility for clearing them up, owning up to pain one may have wittingly or unwittingly caused, is not easy, but it is a tremendous step forward in women's relationships. It enables the valuable and irreplaceable things that occur between women to be strengthened. It moves the relationships out of the murky area of the merged attachment into cleaner more direct lines of communication. It enables the skills women have developed for nurturing, for empathy, for understanding—the giving which is so much a part of a woman's experience of herself—to emerge out of a sense of selfhood and a separated attachment rather than a merged attachment. We need to bravely look at and confront the difficulties that occur between women. We don't need to retreat from them; they are not insurmountable. Our nurturing skills and the genuine love we have for one another stand us in good stead as we take new steps in our relationships.

Chapter 8

Speaking Up

The kinds of difficulties between women that we have been discussing are frequently exacerbated by our hesitation to talk about our feelings of envy, competition, abandonment, anger, guilt, and betrayal. Although many women are extremely practiced at talking about how their partners, their children, their mothers, their fathers, their bosses have annoyed or hurt them, they are novices when it comes to talking *directly* with a friend about an upset or a hurt between them. The mere idea of mentioning a hurt, expressing a grievance, showing a friend that she has made one angry or perhaps asking for something from a woman friend in a straightforward manner, can make a woman very nervous.

She may fret for hours about how to bring up a particular situation. She may talk through whatever is troubling her with another friend. She may hope that her friend will see what has transpired and repair it without her having to bring it up. She may pray for her anger or negative feelings to dissipate, so that she doesn't have to confront her. So unused is she to discussing negative feelings she may have toward a friend that even trivial complaints are rarely expressed in the way that they invariably are when couples quarrel. Often, this doesn't matter at all, for women can swallow the petty annoyances that are bound to occur between them. But because, in general, women are so unaccustomed to speaking up to friends about what may be troubling them, friendships that could be saved deteriorate, causing tremendous heartache and distress.

In our analysis of the root causes of the emotional difficulties between women, we have provided an explanation for why, despite the proliferation of assertiveness training courses and today's emphasis on speaking one's mind, women continue to be hesitant, and barely a dent has been made in this particular area. As we have seen, a central part of what women seek in their relationships with one another is often unconscious. It is no less than the repairing of aspects of the mother-daughter relationship. Women seek support, love, and acceptance from one another. At the same time, they anticipate restriction and rejection. These unconscious wishes and fears are an important part of woman-to-woman relationships. And because a merged attachment so often entwines women's relationships, the feelings between them can become so intense, the need for one another so strong, and the transferences so deep, that it can feel too threatening to bring up difficulties.

For all these reasons then, women rarely develop the facility of talking directly to one another about difficulties between them. Yet, it is imperative that we do so, for if we can share with our friends more of what we feel with them—if we can accept and show that we are angry from time to time, that on occasion we are upset or disappointed, that we do feel abandoned or let down, that we suffer guilt about one another, we can have a richer exchange and better relationships. If we don't bring up our difficulties with one another, we either remain stuck in a merged attachment or the relationship becomes fractured. We develop fantasies about what is actually occurring, reading rejection, abandonment, and anger when these do not exist. We watch one another to assess what the other may be feeling rather than articulating our own feeling or worry. In a sense we remove a part of the self from the relationship, taking the problem into our head where it works out differently, without having confirmed whether it couldn't work differently in real life. We become distanced from one another or cut off from parts of ourselves. Meanwhile, the real relationship contracts and diminishes.

Speaking up is not based on a moral imperative to be honest; it has the more crucial function, potentially, to challenge the projections we may well be making. Projections are a transaction in which, without realizing it, one sees (projects) a part of oneself in the other. We describe another's behavior or translate another's behavior either based on what we wish to be doing but can't see ourselves doing (we imagine they are angry when we are unable to express our own anger), or we load on to them responses from our past that may not be appropriate (we are angry and we imagine they will cut us off if we express it). Such projections limit relationships. The other person becomes less a person in her own right and rather more a vehicle for one's own fantasies and thoughts.

If, however, we speak directly, express a strong feeling, or ask a friend about something we are worried about within the relationship, we intrude on the projection. We allow ourselves to be in the relationship rather than retreating into a fantasy. And in breaking through the isolation and reengaging in the relationship, something else is occurring too: a chink is created in the merged attachment. For when differences or upsets can be spoken about, and insofar as the articulation of differences or negative feelings can be accepted, differentiation has occurred. Let's take a really simple example. Two close women friends, Beth and Nanci, both teachers in their forties, are discussing a third woman in the department, Georgina. Nanci likes going out with Georgina, who she feels is salty and cheeky, full of spunk and energy. Beth, who is also very energetic and outgoing, doesn't trust Georgina. Beth thinks that Georgina is ambitious and manipulative, and tries to prove to Nanci how unreliable Georgina is. Nanci doesn't try to argue about Georgina, she just says, "That's not how I find her. I like her very much." Beth keeps hammering away at Nanci about how dreadful Georgina is until Nanci eventually says, "Look, I'm sorry we feel differently about this, but we do and I'm afraid you'll just have to accept it. I like her and you don't."

Nanci was able to hold her own, neither denying her positive feelings for Georgina, nor trying to change Beth's mind either. Beth had to accept that they didn't always feel the same. This made her a little uneasy. She would much rather that they agreed about Georgina, but at the same time, Nanci's refusal gave her an opportunity to examine the intensity of her wish for the two of them to be in agreement. Beth realized that she had wanted Nanci's agreement because she felt her reality was threatened if it wasn't confirmed by someone else. She distrusted her own feelings unless they seemed to be the same as her friends, and she had pushed Nanci hard on this one not only because she disliked Georgina but because she couldn't quite accept that her dislike was justified unless her best friend agreed. When best friends can disagree even over a relatively simple issue such as this, there is an opportunity for the psychological basis of the relationship to shift from one that encompasses a merged attachment where there is guilt about differences to one in which two women can individuate and connect with one another on that basis.

Sally was feeling very insecure. Her last child had just left home and she was at a bit of a loss. She wasn't sure how to structure her life anymore. Her close friend Joan didn't seem to have much time for her. Sally was sure that it was her neediness that had pushed Joan away. When Sally finally brought up to Joan how upset and hurt she was in general and how Joan's lack of attention had made her feel rejected, Joan was stunned. She had been so caught up in her own difficulties that she hadn't had a clue that Sally was upset. She felt very bad that she had been so remiss toward her friend. She apologized for being distracted and assured Sally that it was her own family crises and preoccupations at work that were distracting her. It took great courage for Sally to bring this up to Joan for she was sure that Joan would confirm her own fantasies. But when she didn't, when Joan said she felt sorry that she had been so unavailable, and that she wasn't put off by how miserable Sally was, both women felt considerably strengthened: Sally, by being able to cancel her fantasy that it was her upset that had pushed Joan away, and Joan, by feeling a genuine compassion and regret that she hadn't been more available to Sally. She could say this without feeling guilty and without feeling put upon by Sally, for instead of Sally accusing Joan of neglect, she spoke directly of her own pain and her own needs. Joan simply felt an obligation to be honest, not to be the all-providing mother who could or could not make things all better.

In short, the outcome of Sally speaking up was reassuring and worthwhile. It broke Sally's feelings of isolation and brought the two of them closer.

Let's look now at another simple example. This is a more complex instance of projection than that between Sally and Joan that shows how speaking up enabled a relationship—and the women in it—to grow rather than collapse.

Alison and Jill are both single and in their twenties. They became friends while working together as secretaries for the Board of Education where they have shared an office for three years. Alison is an extremely sharp, meticulous dresser from manicure to matching shoes. When Jill first met Alison she marveled at her ability to look so good every day. Jill was neat and well-dressed, but never thought about all the finishing touches that add so much to an outfit. In a way, Jill felt that engaging in such details meant one was vain, yet she admired Alison's appearance. After working with Alison for several months, Jill began to polish her nails. She liked it so much that she bought herself many different colors and manicured herself regularly. Gradually, over time, Jill found herself buying colorful scarves, necklaces, and stylish shoes. In the three years that she had known Alison, Jill's appearance radically changed.

Something attracted Jill to Alison's style. It spoke to

a part of Jill that was either unformed or dormant. In seeing Alison's ability to physically present herself in that way, Jill felt a kind of permission to try it herself. Alison both shaped and legitimized Jill's desire. It was within the merged attachment—that is, the mirroring of Alison—that Jill was able to develop herself. Eventually, Jill's style was actually quite different from Alison's, but that distinction was a stage which had to evolve out of the earlier mirror stage.

The difficulties began between them when Jill started to feel some hostility from Alison. Originally, Jill felt that Alison was very supportive of Jill's new interest in her appearance. Alison told Jill about some stores that she liked and they went shopping together on their lunch hours. At the point at which Jill was really beginning to feel good about herself, and that her appearance reflected some of the positive things she felt about herself, she felt that Alison was distant. When she asked Alison questions either about work or personal matters she felt that Alison replied abruptly and coldly. She began to sense a feeling of competition from Alison and noticed that Alison was buying new things and not showing them to Jill and not inviting her to go shopping. Jill was convinced that as long as she was not a threat to Alison, Alison could be friendly but that once Jill, too, looked attractive that Alison could only be competitive with her.

It was true that Alison had become less involved with Jill and she was feeling guilty about it. Another woman who had once worked in the same office, but had been working elsewhere for the past two years, had recently returned and she was spending more time with her. But Jill's interpretation of Alison's behavior had not taken this into account. Her fantasies about what was going on between the two of them reflected the crossroads she had approached in her self-development. Mirroring Alison had been enormously important to her. Copying Alison's clothes was, on a psychological level, merging with another woman. It represented her need for attachment and approval. Her new clothes reflected her sexuality and adult womanhood. It was a break with her mother's view of her and she could only make this break by attaching herself elsewhere (to Alison).

As long as she was getting the approval of another woman she could feel connected and therefore safe. Moving to the next place, of diverging from Alison's taste in clothes, was a manifestation of her individuating. It was a statement of her own development and security within herself, but this was a big step psychologically and she became frightened. She handled her fear by projecting disapproval and prohibitions onto Alison, inventing a scenario in which it was Alison who cut her off from her new independence. The possibility of having her*self* and still having the permission, connection, and love of another woman seemed impossible.

The conflicts that Jill experienced, which originated in her relationship with her mother, were projected onto Alison. Jill felt that she could not become an adult sexual woman without threatening her connection to a woman she was close to. What could Jill do to try to dispel the impression she had? How might she initiate a conversation with Alison?

JILL. Alison, I've been wondering about something. Is there something wrong, because you don't seem to want to spend much time with me?

ALISON. Well, actually I've been aware of it too, but, well, I felt that you've been mad at me for some reason.

JILL. I haven't been angry at you. I've missed you. You've been spending a lot more time with Mary recently. I feel like you haven't wanted me to be around much . . . why have you thought I've been angry?

ALISON. You've acted sort of snippy and annoyed recently.

JILL. Have I? I'm sorry. I don't know why. It's strange. I was sure you were angry with me and you've been thinking I'm angry with you. I thought maybe you didn't like something I did or the way I behaved.

ALISON. I have felt funny about Mary coming back myself and wondered whether the three of us would all get along together, and maybe I've felt I wanted to keep you both for myself.

When Jill reflected on what Alison said, she saw that she had been acting snippy and annoyed. Unconsciously, she was relating to Alison as if Alison were her mother. Alison's nervousness about how to integrate her two friendships and Jill's snippiness were responsible for the distance between the two of them. Alison felt unsure and unentitled about having two friends, as though she were being disloyal to each and so she cut herself off from Jill. Jill had needed to protect herself from Alison because she had being trying to preserve her new self and keep it away from her "mom." In talking to Alison, Jill dispelled her fantasy that Alison disapproved of her growing self-confidence.

As soon as Jill had the courage to talk to Alison about what was happening between them, the connection was reaffirmed and actually strengthened. Alison really appreciated and admired Jill for speaking up. Although Alison had felt nervous throughout the conversation, and she was left with quite a bit to think about, she was excited and happy afterward and her interest in Jill increased.

Often broaching difficult issues such as the coolness between Jill and Alison can bring about good results. Although it is a scary thing to do, it can reignite a relationship that is in danger of disintegrating out of misunderstanding and the unconscious projections that have occurred.

But, it could be argued, these instances of speaking up illustrate fairly simple difficulties that have to be broached. What if there is a genuine growing apart as with Christine and Andrea, strong feelings of envy as we saw with Hilary and her colleagues, feelings of abandonment and betrayal as we saw with Margaret and Adeline. Surely it is pointless and too dangerous to expose these kinds of feelings? What is to be gained by doing so?

The first point to be made is that until the mess of issues that can come between friends is aired, it isn't possible to know whether what is occurring is a jumble of projections, disappointments, and anger because of unreasonable expectations within the friendship, or a genuine growing apart. As we become accustomed to talking with our friends about the difficulties that come between us, we can sort through these issues and if it emerges that the relationship has become untenable, then it is possible to leave it—with sorrow and regret perhaps—but without enormous guilt or conflict. In talking about difficulties or perceptions of the other, it is obviously crucial to find a language and a way of talking that is sensitive and useful to both people.

It is important to find a way to talk about the difficulties that does not engender guilt in the other or impose demands that are essentially unmeetable. There is a world of difference between telling a friend you felt let down and *accusing* her of letting you down. Telling a friend that you are angry is more constructive than exploding on her. Because women are so unaccustomed to talking directly with their women friends in this way, it is bound to be bumpy at first. We will say the wrong things, or present our grievances and upsets awkwardly. But this has to happen in order for the silences and discomforts we live with to dissipate. One of the most damaging effects of the silences is that we forget how very helpful and healing our relationships with women can be. We lose sight of the capabilities our friends have to help us through our muddles. The richness we so value in our woman-to-woman friendships recedes and we have a distorted view of what it is that—when we weren't angry, disappointed, hurt—so attracted us to a particular friend. When one of Hilary's colleagues in the Chicago Psychology Research Center told her how envious she was of the attention and exposure her work was receiving, that she didn't hate her but wanted what Hilary had for herself, Hilary was able to talk about Brenda's important work on postpartum depression and how it could become more widely disseminated. Hilary could help Brenda see that her work was very good, that it was the capriciousness of the media that had seized on her own work on child abuse and that it wasn't, in this case, anything intrinsic in Hilary that her work had received so much exposure.

Hilary supported Brenda's wish to have her work better known and used. Brenda was happy to have Hilary's support and Hilary was relieved that with Brenda she was no longer the object of envy. Hilary didn't have to try to deny that she was getting attention or deny that she was enjoying it. She could have her experience and she could recognize Brenda's. If they hadn't spoken directly, Hilary would have continued to feel guilty while Brenda would have used Hilary's public prominence to explain why she wasn't getting more of what she wanted.

Unlike many marriages or committed sexual relationships in which arguments may expose negative feelings, many friendships flounder amid unspoken disagreements, hurts, and misunderstandings. Arguments between girlfriend and boyfriend, between husband and wife are considered healthy. But as we have seen, in friendship such feelings are rarely directly expressed to the person who engendered them. There is a hesitation in being frank about feelings which may suggest that there has been some unkindness, lack of thoughtfulness, or selfishness on the part of a friend. Exposing feelings that suggest difference, a wanting for oneself (as opposed to giving to the other), or the desire for a separate experience, can be excruciating between friends. Wanting something for oneself rather than offering to share it with a friend feels selfish, abandoning, a feeling to be tucked away rather than exposed.

Rosalie, Terry, and Donna had been very close friends in art college. After college Donna got a terrific job in a new museum that was opening in Los Angeles. Rosalie and Terry both stayed in their hometown of New York, one to paint, the other to work in furniture design. Despite the geographic separation, they continued to think of themselves as a threesome. Phone calls were frequent. Rosalie and Terry always talked about Donna, shared their opinions about her latest lovers, how her job was going, and so on. One Christmas when Donna returned to New York for a visit, Rosalie and Terry picked her up at the airport and the three women spent the first evening together and all of the next day.

The following evening Rosalie took Donna aside and confessed to her that she wanted to spend some time during the week's visit alone with her. She said she loved the three of them being together but that she wanted some time with just the two of them. Donna agreed. At the end of the evening they all discussed plans for the following day and suddenly there was an awkward silence. Rosalie looked at Donna; Donna looked at Rosalie. Rosalie said that there was a photography exhibit that she thought Donna would enjoy and suggested that she and Donna go and then meet up with Terry in the afternoon. There was another awkward silence. They all agreed that would be the plan, said goodnight, and went home.

On the way home Terry felt awful. She felt furious with Rosalie. How could Rosalie be so insensitive as to not invite her along to the exhibit? How thoughtless, or worse than that even, how mean of her. She felt excluded, abandoned, and angry.

Rosalie went home shaking, knowing that Terry was upset and feeling that it was awful to have excluded her. Rosalie didn't see how she could enjoy the time alone with Donna after this. She considered telephoning them both to change the plan.

Donna returned to her parents' house feeling anxious and tense. These visits were always so mixed. She loved seeing her friends but organizing her time between friends and family seemed to turn into such a mess. It always seemed that everyone was tugging at her and that someone would be angry with her for not giving enough. Now it had happened with Terry. She wanted to telephone her to talk about it but she didn't know what to say.

As long as Rosalie, Donna, and Terry were together, all was well. If they remained a group, a threesome, each felt secure in her place. Rosalie's stated desire to spend time alone with Donna challenged the merged three-way attachment. It created a boundary of individuation where before there had been none. This was threatening and upsetting for each of them in different ways. Terry's exclusion made her feel angry and competitive with Rosalie. Rosalie felt greedy and infantile, guilty for wanting too much. Her efforts to get what she wanted left her feeling that she had done something wrong. Because she had felt unsure about whether it was all right for her to pursue what she wanted, she had become sneaky. Donna felt guilty for following her own desires in the first place and choosing to live in California. During her return visits, she felt she should be available to everyone and fill all their needs. In California, she felt much more sure of herself, whereas in New York with friends and family she automatically returned to her merged attachments. She wasn't even aware of her own need to be with either of her friends separately. When people's needs were confluent, she was fine, but when a divergence was expressed she felt torn, anxious, and guilty. She could not choose and she couldn't cope with the idea that someone might be left out and hurt.

Although these three good friends could each imagine having a conversation in twosomes about the awkwardness caused by the situation, it was outside their experience to imagine all three talking together about the difficulty. Indeed, each of them wanted to call the others, but at first *only to change the situation back, to make it more comfortable, to re-create the merged attachment.* Each felt so wrong in her own upset and so ashamed of her own feelings that she did not feel able to share them with her dearest friends.

As it happened, Rosalie did call Donna. Initially, Donna thought that maybe they should include Terry, but as they talked together more, they both realized that for the two of them not to spend the morning together alone was ridiculous. When they had all lived in New York, the threesome had frequently divided into twosomes according to their different interests. Rosalie felt better that Donna could also assert what she wanted, and that she wasn't forced to take all the responsibility for wanting to spend time alone; neither was she cast as the rejecting person. Donna was pleased to recognize that she did have her own wishes and wasn't just responsive to the tug of the threesome. Then Rosalie called Terry. At first, Terry was a bit distant on the phone, and Rosalie nearly got cold feet. She thought perhaps she should just bury the whole idea and abandon her trip with Donna. But she didn't. Since she could easily imagine how Terry was feeling, she was able to approach the difficulty with considerable compassion. She said that this was a situation that was always going to come up for the three of them when Donna was in town for only a limited time. She said she could understand that Terry might have felt hurt and rejected, but that she really did want to spend some time separately with Donna. Terry listened and tried to get past her hurt feelings. She realized that it was a perfectly legitimate wish on Donna and Rosalie's part. She herself wouldn't mind spending an evening alone with Donna, but she hadn't even allowed herself to consider the possibility.

In this encounter, Rosalie's two initiatives—first in expressing her desire to be alone with Donna and then in telephoning Donna and Terry—pushed the friendship forward to a different level. In asserting herself, she gave each of them an opportunity to grow; to see that the relationship was strong enough to survive and accommodate different needs. Nobody collapsed under the weight of guilt, nobody's pain was denied, nobody's conflicts went unrecognized. The real situation with its attendant difficulties was managed.

Resolution was considerably more difficult for Christine, the kindergarten teacher and Andrea, the law student whom we met in chapter 4. As you may recall, what each one sought in the friendship shifted, making the original basis of the friendship untenable. During their friendship, Andrea changed. When she had first become friendly with Christine, she had been quite unhappy and pessimistic. She and Christine had spent a lot of time commiserating with one another and agreeing that life is terrible. But as time went on, Andrea's self-confidence developed and she began to have a different outlook on life. She felt dragged down by Christine and found herself arguing about Christine's negativity. Christine, meanwhile, felt jealous of Andrea's new friend Julie, and confused by Andrea's rejection of her. What could these two friends have done that might have produced a less painful end to their friendship? Whatever was said, wouldn't the friendship have died anyway? Why make the process even more graphic and painful?

The fact is we don't know what would have happened if, instead of Andrea retreating and Christine pursuing her, the two of them had been able to talk about what was happening between them. We can't be sure that there would have been a different outcome, but there is a reasonable chance that even if the relationship had ended anyway, its demise would have been better understood and the hurt and confusion lessened. If they had been able to talk about what was happening between them, Andrea might have been able to say that she was feeling more hopeful and optimistic these days. Christine might have been able to say she felt rejected. If that reality were acknowledged by each of them, they might have been able to go on to acknowledge that Christine felt abandoned and Andrea's new confidence threatened her. Andrea might have discussed how fragile her new confidence sometimes seemed and how Christine's pessimism frightened her, for it felt like it might draw her backwards. This, in turn, would have opened up a conversation about the dynamic within their relationship in which they had, as we saw, raged against the world together while simultaneously denying or externalizing their own pain. In other words, Andrea and Christine would have needed to address the way in which Christine continued to see herself only as a victim.

In doing so, they might have been able to understand how seeing herself as a victim trapped Christine and kept her stuck in her unhappiness and feelings of powerlessness. They might have explored how Andrea had overcome this in herself, and how and why she sometimes still felt she was on shaky ground. If they had been able to talk with one another about Christine's unhappiness as opposed to only raging at the external injustice that was causing it, Christine could have been directly in touch with her pain. The reader may well ask why removing the defense is worthwhile, why is it better to be in pain than to feel oneself to be a victim?

It is very hard to move out of a victim psychology—and the unremittingly awful feelings that surround one—unless one discovers what it shields. When that emerges, it is more likely that change can take place, and that the fantasies—of everything always being either utterly hopeless until the metaphorical white knight arrives—that accompany being a victim, can be jettisoned in favor of coming to terms directly with the unhappiness. In facing her unhappiness, Christine could have developed a certain confidence. Andrea would have been able to feel compassion and empathy for her rather than being turned off by her defense.

This, of course, is the most promising outcome that could have occurred. It is entirely possible that in trying to speak with one another about what was happening between them, Christine would have raged at Andrea for abandoning her and confirmed her sense of herself as a victim. Andrea would have felt guilty and treacherous. The relationship would have broken up with no real gain. But this outcome, although possible, was not that likely, for although their friendship had included a dynamic in which their merged attachment kept out pain, they also cared very much about one another, they had been friends for a long time, they had many things in common, and they had liked each other a lot. The positive aspects of their friendship may well have counterbalanced the upset, once the upset had been expressed, rather than necessitated the end of the relationship.

Andrea and Christine's friendship broke down because Andrea was unable to go along with or challenge Christine's negative view of everything since she was no longer so negative herself.

Perhaps because Adeline and Margaret were social workers and somewhat accustomed to examining psychological processes, the conversation they were eventually able to have about Margaret's further training at a psychoanalytic institute touched on the psychodynamics operating for each of them and between them. One evening shortly after Margaret had been accepted into the training program, they went out together and talked about what this development meant in Margaret's life and the kinds of questions raised for Adeline. Adeline explained how threatened she felt, how she feared losing Margaret, and how she had felt the urge to apply too. Margaret told Adeline how apprehensive she had felt, that she imagined Adeline might be critical or feel jealous. They were both relieved that these feelings were out in the open. There was nothing to do about them, but airing them brought the friends closer. They talked about how Adeline's background had made her feel somewhat insecure about her choices and how Margaret's leaving social work made her feel shaky. They talked about how their backgrounds allowed each of them to feel or not feel entitled to further education and career advancement, and so on. Most importantly, they talked about the ways in which they were very close and committed to each other and how they wanted their bond to survive this radical change. In talking, it became clearer to Adeline that she did not want to change her job. She was happy in social work and although Margaret's becoming a psychotherapist would be a real loss for her, it wasn't what she wanted for herself. Margaret was able to describe to Adeline how she was both scared and excited to leave the security of an institutional setting. Part of what made her feel able to do so was the love and support she had always received from Adeline. It had helped her to feel stronger in herself and seek new avenues for work.

Because Adeline and Margaret could talk, they could share their nervousness with one another. Training at the institute was a big step for Margaret and it would mean a change in their relationship, but they could see that it might also enrich their friendship, not threaten it. Through the love and support they had given each other in the past, they had helped each other grow up emotionally in significant ways. Although their friendship had elements of a merged attachment (i.e., the panic that almost impelled Adeline to apply to the psychoanalytic institute too) they had managed over the years to use it, if you like, to heal themselves, to find the consistent nurturance and approval they had both so needed from another woman. Having given each other so much, they were now able to differentiate and to keep a strong attachment based on their psychological separateness. They did not need to retreat back into a merged attachment.

The merged attachment that cements relationships, preventing the discussion of difficult feelings that might occur between women, also acts as a brake on women discussing aspects of one another's lives. Many women have discussed with us the frustration they feel when they rush to concur with a friend's perception of a situation, while inside themselves they have a different view of things. Other women have disclosed their own unease with not being challenged enough by girlfriends, even though they don't relish confrontation. Such problems revolve around the issue of commiseration. Commiseration is an integral part of women's highly developed repertoire of giving. Commiseration is the capacity to show that one understands what another might be feeling and comforting her or him, often by producing instances in which one has been similarly made to feel hurt/angry/irritated/betrayed, and so on. Feeling another's support in this way can be very reassuring. The sympathy and concern, the sharing of experience can help one feel less isolated. Simultaneously, however, if the commiseration is built on an identification with the other, i.e., one actually feels what one's friend is feeling as though in her shoes, then the sympathy isn't helpful to the person in pain. What do we mean by this?

As we have seen, women's overpowering need for one another and the merger and identification that is a feature of women's friendships brings both rich contact and immediacy to the relationship at the same time that it may preclude or silence differences. In commiserating, we are not simply having a good moan together. There is often an implicit demand to see the situation as it is presented and not to question the other person's perceptions. Commiserating, then, can mean that one is immobilized and complying with a view that doesn't feel accurate. A typical scenario with much commiseration occurs when girlfriends discuss their difficulties with their partners. Often, one will say to the other, "I know just what you mean," and go on to detail the irritations in her own relationship. Much time together may be spent in this way, providing a kind of mutual support system. In reality, however, there is nothing supportive in confirmation of a dreary and pessimistic view of things. The support they give one another reinforces the sense that it is "him" who is at fault and there is little to be done about it except to complain together.

"He" may well be at fault, but if the woman cannot accept the way he behaves and if he is unwilling or unable to change his offending behavior or attitude, then friends may have a greater role to play than simply to commiserate. Often it is possible to see that one's friend misperceives a situation. One might see a pattern of responses in her sexual relationship that contributes to the difficulty. Often the friend is looking for something beyond an empathic response or confirmation of her own view. Her own view has clearly not helped change the situation and it may be that her view requires a challenge. In such circumstance, the commiseration prevents an honest reappraisal.

Greta, a booking clerk in a theatrical agency, frequently moaned to Jane, one of the secretaries there, about how awful and inconsiderate her husband Paul was. Jane was very sympathetic, and although she and her boyfriend had had their share of difficult times, she felt generally optimistic about her own relationship. She listened to Greta and the two of them concocted things that might induce a different response in him, but to little avail. He was inconsiderate and thoughtless and as a result he often hurt Greta. Greta, in turn, would feel rejected and become clingy, wanting some proof of his love to counterbalance his distance and meanness. They alternated between squabbles and private wars. None of the suggestions that Jane and Greta thought up together had much impact in practice, partly because Greta was too unsure of herself to try them out consistently and partly because Paul wasn't open to changing. In time,

Jane dreaded that moment in the conversation when Greta would detail the latest outrage on Paul's part or the latest instance of hurt. It made her feel as helpless as Greta. At the same time, she wondered why Greta was so stuck in the marriage. There were no children, Greta was self-supporting, and the relationship was clearly unsatisfying.

One day when Jane and Greta were out for coffee, Jane found that she could not contain herself any longer and when Greta started to moan about Paul, Jane said simply, "Maybe we should think about your part in this, there must be a reason why you stay with him." Stating this in such a direct manner brought Greta up short and made her think about it. In the ensuing conversation, Greta talked about how she really didn't expect any better; her parents' marriage had been awful, her own relationship with her mother and father fraught. She had no expectation that things could work out better with Paul, or anyone for that matter. It was very distressing for Greta to face these feelings in herself but as she and Jane talked together some of the upset about how hopeless she felt was expressed and discharged. Revealing her most intimate feelings to Jane made her feel stronger. Having the feelings listened to and understood made her feel a little more optimistic.

Because Jane didn't reject her or try to cover her pain with false solutions to what was evidently a much deeper problem, Greta felt some calmness. She went through a period in which she was quite depressed. Although there was no immediate improvement in her marriage, she did stop waiting for Paul to press the magic button that would make her life turn out better. The energy used to keep this unconscious fantasy alive in her and to dispense the rage that resulted when she was inevitably disappointed, now became more available for other purposes. Gradually, she found herself reaching out to other relationships in which she did feel regarded and cared for.

By doing more than commiserating, Jane helped Greta to mobilize strengths that had become dormant during the marriage. Commiseration is an example of a skill women have developed which has both positive and negative aspects to it. Women's identifications with one another provide them with the capacity to understand and sometimes even feel what another is experiencing. This can bring great comfort, intimacy, and contact between women. But as we have seen, this capacity often stems from the woman's search for a sense of self through an identification and merger with someone else. In other words, she is able to feel what another is feeling because her own boundaries and her own feelings are so malleable. If this malleability is at work when she is commiserating, she may be so imbued with feeling what another is feeling, sensing what another may be fearing, or knowing what the other person is repressing, that she is unable to give of herself as a separate person. By being in tune with someone else in this way, she has abdicated herself and cannot usefully contest and challenge the other person's experience. As such, she is not really being as good a friend as she might be.

Commiseration and the allied phenomena of distorting one's own experience ever so slightly to fit in with that of a friend's, occurs so habitually between women, that even in apparently trivial exchanges, it can be very difficult to not do so. But it can be important to find a different response to a friend's upset, especially in

Freida's case where, as we have seen, she was struggling hard to free herself from always seeing things from the other person's point of view. When Melinda moaned about how awful the weather was on holiday, Freida was tempted to act as she had unthinkingly in the past and to moan that something was amiss on her holiday too. She felt pulled to commiserate based on a shared experience even when there wasn't one. She wanted to say, "I know, I know, my holiday was only so-so," but that wasn't accurate, her holiday had been wonderful. She had been tempted to deny her experience to support her friend in pain; if they both had a bad time, then all would be right. She felt pulled to give out of the merged attachment where everything was the same. But as we have seen, giving out of the merged attachment in which one's own experience is denied actually prevents real giving. Freida would have had to tell a white lie about her holiday in order to join with Melinda. Freida found a more satisfactory response for both her and Melinda by being genuinely sympathetic, hearing how disappointed Melinda was without having to bring in a similar manufactured experience. Precisely because she had had a good holiday she could appreciate how important that was and she was genuinely compassionate that things had not worked out well for Melinda. This simple example was important to Freida in many ways. Her own struggle for authenticity was confirmed. Although from the outside it may not have seemed significant, inside Freida it was a building block in her asserting herself rather than collapsing into someone else's experience.

The wish to speak up, the need to speak up, and the fear of speaking up are present in so many of women's relationships with one another. But the effort is more than worthwhile. It not only clarifies difficulties in the relationships and allows the individuals to sort through the tangles and projections that exist; it almost always pushes the relationships forward to a deeper, more satisfying level. The exhilaration two women feel after they talk with each other about feelings, desires, or upsets they felt ashamed of, is always surprising. Before the difficulty is aired, there is a kind of cloud over the friendship that blots out the very positive parts of the relationship, creating in each of the women a kind of amnesia about why they had even liked the person in the first place. When they talk through their difficult feelings— and most often are not rejected as anticipated—they feel excited and strengthened individually and in their friendship. All this can happen because this is not an encounter in honesty per se or a mandate to "tell it like it is." It is because the compassion each woman can find in herself toward the other woman, even though she is hurt or angry, or the respect she can muster for herself, requiring her to bring up something that disturbed her, allows her to present her case from her point of view. "This is how I see it. Is this how you see it?" This starting point avoids encounters that, under the guise of talking straight, are attacks of one kind or another. And this perhaps is the key. To share the distress that may be engendered in a relationship, the person initiating the talk has to say what *she* experiences and what *she* has been imagining is the situation for the other person. It is not her place to say what is for the other person, to either interpret or accuse them. She should endeavor to say, "I felt jealous," "I felt envious," "This circumstance made me angry," rather than accusing the other of making her envious, angry, or whatever. In other words, the woman needs to recognize that her friend may not have done anything to attack her; her friend's actions more likely have to do with her friend. She must also recognize that the feelings aroused in her, as we saw in earlier chapters, may be a defense against other feelings. These are feelings which women friends can help each other with. Expressing things from one's own vantage point helps to clarify whatever is troubling and to open that up to another without purposefully provoking guilt or anger. It is important that women learning to talk with one another in this new and frank way find a language and a form that takes account of their love and need for one another. We must trust that speaking up to our women friends will not sever the ties, but only strengthen them.

Chapter 9

Friends and Lovers

The seven members of the Chicago psychologists collective we met in chapter 5 take out their diaries to make a date for a meeting. A variety of thoughts, reactions, and feelings occur to each woman as she looks in her datebook. But those of them who are in couples share a difficult problem—how to reconcile their commitment to their women friends and colleagues with their commitment to their couple relationship. Rena has recently started living with her boyfriend and hesitates about evening activities that conflict with being with him. Ann and Susanne, who each have young children, envision telling their partners that for yet another evening they will be left to attend to the domestic responsibilities on their own. Brenda lives with her lover, Jill, who consistently feels angry about Brenda's devotion to her work, feeling that more energy and time are given to the group than to their relationship. Brenda imagines telling Jill about the meeting and anticipates the tension that will follow.

After the initial reactions each woman in a couple begins to make the internal adjustments necessary to bring her*self* back into the picture. And as she connects with her own desire and genuine interest in the meeting, she feels the pulls even more acutely. She quickly makes a mental note of her partner's schedule for that week. Those with children mentally juggle babysitting; those without children suggest a night they know their partner is busy. For each, the attachments to friends and partner seem at odds. The friendship is experienced as a pull on the relationship and vice versa. Even for these feminist psychologists, who can lecture on women's psychology and women's difficulties with entitlement or autonomous desire, there is lingering guilt, a feeling of selfishness about taking so much for herself, for overindulging, for wanting both. She imagines that her partner will have a negative reaction to her other attachment, and often she is correct.

At the height of the women's movement, none of these women would have predicted this dilemma. Indeed, one of the great breakthroughs of the early seventies was women's realization of the importance of relationships with women friends and colleagues. No more, we declared, would we drop our closest female friends the moment a man called. As we encouraged each other to pursue our desires, we could not conceive of the consequences this might have on the time available to spend with friends. We didn't know we were gradually shifting our priorities. We didn't know that a few years down the line weeks could go by without our spending time with our dearest woman friend. And yet, women are, once again, it seems, prioritizing their couple relationships and seeing less of their women friends.

How did this happen? Is it simply that we grew up and moved from one phase of our lives to another? Have we, in fact, reproduced exactly what our mothers and grandmothers experienced before us? Has the transition from college years with all its passion and intensity to mature adult life followed its inevitable course? Maybe we were right all along when we thought that when one reached thirty, it was all over. Could it be that the intensity of our female friendships was merely a phase which is now over?

We think not. What has happened is not an inevitable part of growing older, or even an unavoidable result of having so many other time- and energy-consuming commitments in our lives. Certainly these are all real constraints and difficulties to overcome, but we believe that more is going on. Once again, underlying psychological forces are at work, forces derived from what it means to be a woman in our society.

To some extent it is possible to see the reassertion of the priority of the couple relationship as a retreat from the difficulties encountered in women's friendships. As we have seen, the very intensity of women's relationships, the importance we have allowed them, together with the very real social changes for women over the past decade have, in turn, produced new and difficult tensions between women. In the preceding chapters, we saw why it can seem easier to retreat from these emotional issues than to confront them. A byproduct of what seemed like the impossibility of speaking up to our women friends about these unsettling feelings was often a retreat back into heterosexual and couple relationships. By spending more time within the couple, we could sidestep the feelings of envy, competition, longing, and disappointment that we felt toward a woman friend. It was a lot easier to tell our male partner about our annoyances and irritations with a girlfriend than to tell her directly. Now, rather than finding oneself telling a girlfriend about the grievances we felt toward a male partner, it is often the other way around. And we feel surprised and relieved that men can listen to these feelings and offer support of one kind or another.

Although many of the the dynamics we shall address here occur in both lesbian and heterosexual relationships, gender difference makes those dynamics far more obvious. For this reason, we have chosen to focus on heterosexual relationships.

Our relationships with men, who are obviously a different gender, seem to offer the possibility of breaking free of merged attachments. Male-female relationships *appear* to provide the woman with the sense of differentiation and separateness that she seeks. For all its uncertainties and misunderstandings, the couple relationship is, in important psychological ways, a necessary and safe place for many women. Squabbles, fights, and disagreements are more accepted in couple relationships than in friendships. Unlike a friendship, a marriage is not in jeopardy (even if it feels like it at the moment) because the partners argue. Although friends may disagree, feel disappointed in one another, or angry, dealing with those feelings seems far more difficult. Although women may feel enraged by their sexual partner's different point of view, the experience of being challenged, of being forced to take account of different opinions, of not having one's insights automatically concurred with, is part of the psychological attraction that men hold for women. We've seen how difficult it is for women to create this kind of boundary between each other and yet how crucial it is to do so.

This is not to paint too rosy a picture of marriage, for many women are trapped in abusive relationships, relationships in which they feel passive, or relationships in which open disagreement is not tolerated. Nor is it to suggest that women are psychologically separate within couple relationships. It is rather to explain one of the buried psychological dynamics that fuel male–female relationships, dynamics that sometimes work as an antidote to a merged attachment. For even though couples merge psychologically every bit as easily as women do, the shape of heterosexual merger is not the same as that of female to female merger.[14]

The essential differences in men's and women's psychologies are important to our discussion in two ways. As we all know, male and female personalities follow in broad terms what is considered—at any given time—appropriate for boys and girls, for men and women. In this process toward selfhood and identity, a woman's interactions with other people provide her with a reference point. She creates and maintains a sense of self through her connections with others. Women live in a network of relationships and know themselves through these relationships. Men, on the other hand, know themselves in the *difference*, i.e., in the way they distinguish themselves from others. The image of the masculine man is attractive to women because it suggests (no matter how mistakenly) the man's ability to be a full and substantial person on his own. Although she cannot easily identify with this image, she may well be drawn to it as a counterpoint to a selfhood that is essentially affiliative.

Similarly, the defense structures of men and women,

the psychological mechanisms that protect the un-developed and hidden parts of each of us, develop differ-ently in childhood for boys and girls.[15] Paramount as a defense structure for men is a kind of false differentia-tion, a setting oneself apart from and free of others. As an infant, the boy is merged with mother and in that merger incorporates aspects of her femininity. In his process of separation-individuation, he utilizes her gen-der difference to delineate the boundaries between them. He comes to know himself through this difference. His developing masculine self is not mother. In his move-ment toward autonomy, he distances himself from mother and femininity and the latter becomes a buried and repressed aspect of his developing self. Later on in life attachment and intimacy in heterosexual relation-ships threaten the false boundaries that were con-structed at a very early point in his psychological development. Thus intimacy, which threatens to touch his buried "feminine" (undifferentiated) self, provokes a fear of the loss of the essentially masculine self he has come to know.

For a woman, we've seen that a lack of boundaries, false or genuine, exists and she is easily subject to merger within her intimate relationships. Indeed, she seeks her identity through attachment. In intimate relationships she can lose a clear sense of herself. Thus, when a man and a woman merge psychologically, they both face a loss of self, but the defense structure that exists against these losses works very differently, so that *typically men crave distance while women crave closeness.* Women uncon-sciously look to men to provide the nurturance we asso-ciate with femininity as well as the separateness and differentiation we associate with masculinity.

Ours may be the first generation in recent history that has begun to make significant emotional demands on men, requiring them to struggle within themselves to develop new resources for emotional contact and intimacy. Men, too, have changed because of feminism and because of their own dissatisfactions with the damaging effects of being raised with a masculine identity. In many ways, some women are beginning to get more emotionally from their relationships with men.

For women with women lovers, the conflict is posed less dramatically. Lesbian relationships benefit from the shared social experience and history between women. Lesbian relationships benefit from the fact that two women have been raised with the capacity to nurture and to care, to initiate emotionally and to be emotionally responsive. Women lovers do not enter a different psychological mode when relating to each other as opposed to relating to their friends. This, combined with the sexual relationship, means that the propensity to implode into a merged attachment is exaggerated. Intimacy may be problematic because the defenses against a loss of self in the merged attachment are in ascendance. Some lesbian women feel that they can maintain a sense of self in their friendships, a sense that may become less clear within their sexual relationships. And yet, as opposed to heterosexual women, often for lesbians the distinctions between friends and lovers are less obviously delineated.

For heterosexual women, the division between what we want from men and what we want from women is no longer as clear-cut as it used to be. Although our mothers may have longed for an emotionally responsive partner, their expectations were quite different from ours. Divorce rates in recent years have proven that unsatisfying marriages are no longer tolerated to the same extent as in previous generations where the significant attachment was made to the man whether or not one actually got the emotional connection one sought. Women today expect more from their emotional relationships with men. The lines of attachment are blurred as the needs we have in our relationships with men and women have overlapped. We desire emotional connection and autonomy from both. And yet, as we've seen, separated attachments are a mystery to us. *Believing that we can achieve our own psychological separateness and maintain our intimate and needed attachments to both a man (or men) and a woman (or women) is almost unfathomable.*

As we've seen, women and men alike are unaccustomed to experiencing women as separate and so assumptions are easily made, in both lesbian and heterosexual relationships, about the life of the couple taking precedence over her autonomous activities. Out of her own need for attachment and her deep belief that it is she who must adapt herself to secure the relationship, the woman adjusts her life outside the couple to fit her partner's needs (or her fantasy of what the partner will accept). Unconsciously, she is busy holding onto the attachment. Her internal world is actively engaged in a juggling act to both maintain her autonomy and not threaten the connection. Sensing the potential disruption, she attempts to preserve the relationship by suppressing, in her partner as well as in herself, the knowledge of her separateness. She acts on an unconscious realization of the parameters of her separateness as she curtails and adapts her activities to fit her partner's.

And so, we have seen a gradual realignment of sexual relationships and friendships. The marriage has become a partnership, a mutual support system that is charged with meeting more of each individual's needs. For some women, this works reasonably well, for others it is a disaster. For women friends who are both in couples, often the couple relationships take over and become the modus operandi for social gatherings. The couples now go out together to dinner, to the movies. If the women had been friends originally, a shift occurs in the kind of quality of time they spend together. Perhaps they make an effort to meet occasionally on their own, but for the most part they find themselves alone only on the telephone or in the ladies' room on an evening out with their husbands. It may be just during those brief moments that they manage to experience the kind of intimate exchange that once filled their lives. They have shifted their dependency on each other to their partners and, in so doing, there is a symmetry in their experience that may seem to work for all parties.

Some women in this situation know that they miss the time with their girlfriend. They feel that something is lacking and they experience a special kind of loneliness. They are aware that relationships with their partners and children fill the better part of their nonworking time and, although they may be very happy in their family situation, a part of them hungers for woman-to-woman contact. Some women make the effort to carve out time for lunch or dinner with a friend, which they then enjoy and savor. Others may experience more tension in negotiating time with girlfriends. They may miss it but are anxious about time away from their partners.

They cannot comfortably and securely socialize outside the couple. Still others grit their teeth and go without, telling themselves that they are not alone and have no real reason to feel the sadness or emptiness they feel. They may experience these hungry or deprived feelings as disappointment with their partner, and they may feel dissatisfied in their couple relationship. Alternatively, many women blame themselves for wanting too much, being too needy, and believe that these emotional yearnings are just another example of their insatiability. But for almost all women, there is some degree of disappointment. Some of their emotional needs go unmet.

A man may be extremely helpful in discussing strategies for a given situation, but he is likely to be rather less fluent in how to initiate or engage in emotional dialogues. He may become irritated by his partner's needs, feeling them as demands upon him, or he may be perplexed by her explosive anger when he fails to adequately understand something she wants from him. In the misunderstanding, she feels utterly frustrated and wants him to understand her just as she imagines a girlfriend would. It is here that we separate another strand in the intricate web of relationships. It is as though *women want women to have the capacity for differentiation that men convey and they want men to have the capacity to identify and have the emotional antenna that women have.* There is a continual search for the attachment that will provide continuity, security, and love while simultaneously providing the boundaries of separateness enabling her to exist in her own right.

However much support and emotional connection a husband or male lover may provide, he cannot replace a woman friend. His experience makes it impossible for him to share and deeply understand some aspects of female experience that a girlfriend understands effortlessly. Girlfriends are able to communicate so easily because of the wide range of their common experience and interests. A couple may go out to dinner and find that they have little to talk about. This *rarely* happens with women friends. As we've seen, women share in nuances, details, and layers of multitextured exchanges.

Moreover, whereas a man can't replace the connectedness of a relationship with another woman, neither can he easily encourage his partner's psychological separateness. No matter how loving and caring a husband or male partner may be, he has tremendous difficulty with the autonomy and separateness of his female partner. There is a complex interaction between women's and men's emotional dependency needs.[16] Although men may appear to be less dependent and more genuinely separate, this is because their emotional dependency needs are more continually satisfied. First their mothers and then their wives and girlfriends—who were raised from day one to see nurturing and caring for others as part of their personality and their duty—provide that kind of care. Thus, by and large, emotional nurturing in heterosexual couples does not occur symmetrically. A woman comes to marriage expecting and yearning for a partner who will understand her deeply, accept her, and be there for her to lean on emotionally, but all too often she finds that her partner is frightened of intimacy, steers away from emotional contact and discussion, and is somewhat frightened or put off by her needs. Whereas, in some sense, her husband continues to receive mothering, she does not. Therefore her unconscious expectations, desire for both a nourishing connection as well as a supported autonomy, is rarely achieved.

Often, a woman receives sufficient nurturance from her women friends and expects very little of it from her partner. Some partners have understood and supported their lovers' desire for time with women friends. They may feel some discomfort when their partners tell them they will be going out with a friend on a given evening, leaving them to fend for themselves, but make efforts to contain their unease. Their own anxiety about their partner's separateness is semiconscious. Rationally they recognize that their partners are autonomous adults who are, indeed, separate from themselves. These men usually have been influenced by the women's movement and know that times have changed, that women should not be expected to be at their beck and call. To one degree or another, they are making personal efforts to examine and change their expectations and assumptions vis-à-vis women.

Some men encourage their partner's friendships because they allow them time for their own work or other interests. They may feel relieved when their mates make a date with a girlfriend, leaving them to meet a friend for a drink, to do some work at home that evening, or to just relax and watch television. One of the things men often find difficult about being married is the loss of the feeling of freedom that they feel they have on their own. But many men feel threatened by their partner's relationships outside the couple. A wife's attachment elsewhere signifies her separateness, and as such engenders discomfort for him. He may feel abandoned and lonely when his partner is not around and it is at these times that he feels his own emotional dependency. He may feel inadequate; if he was enough, his partner would not need to be with others. He may act as if he approves of the friendships but makes it difficult for time to be spent together.

Jerry, a thirty-three-year-old computer consultant, felt quite uncomfortable about his wife's friendships. He saw Elaine's group of friends as strong, talkative, vivacious women. He both admired them and was scared of them. He felt excluded from their closeness, a closeness that he felt, perhaps, was missing in his friendships with other men. He felt awkward when they were around and didn't know how to relate comfortably with them. He would pout when they were around or speak critically about them after spending time with them. Jerry traveled a lot on business trips and knew that during those times Elaine spent most of her free time on dates with her various friends. Once, when he was away, Elaine had a miscarriage. Jerry was upset for her and sad that they wouldn't be having another child right away. But when they spoke on the phone and he learned that Elaine's friend Lenore was looking after her, he turned the conversation to other matters. He felt hurt that Lenore was in his place. After he hung up and thought about it all, he also felt relieved that Lenore was there because he felt that she would be able to handle the situation much better than he could have. The next day when Jerry telephoned and Elaine said she was feeling a bit better, he told her that although he had completed his business he was going to stay for a couple of days to play golf. After all, Elaine was doing fine and her friends were doing a fine job of caring for her. Unconsciously, Jerry acted out his hurt, inadequacy, and imagined rejection by rejecting Elaine. For Jerry, Elaine's attachments outside their couple relationship were extremely difficult to tolerate. He needed her devotion and full-time attention in order to feel safe and relaxed within the relationship. Although Elaine was extremely upset by Jerry's actions, the tension between her marriage and her friendships was an accepted part of their relationship. She was continually juggling these relationships and transporting herself back and forth between two worlds.

The primacy of the couple relationship, then, has left many women feeling, once again, emotionally hungry. We can now see more clearly a current dilemma for women in couples. On the one hand, as they find themselves more enclosed within the couple, part of them is aware of feeling isolated and, at times, alienated from the person to whom they are now closest. On the other hand, the time pressures of work and children, the desire (conscious or unconscious) to avoid the new conflicts and discomforts between women friends, and the psychological construct that has us giving up our attachment to a woman in order to attempt separation, leaves women with an intangible emptiness; an emptiness that, we would suggest, derives from a lack of sufficient time and contact with other women. This emptiness is a painful reminder of some critical aspects of the mother-daughter relationship.

As girls, we were unable to receive both the continuity of connection, love, and acceptance from mother as well as the boundaries of differentiation and psychological separateness. Instead, we left that relationship, burying the pain of what we didn't get. As we've seen, in our relationships with women we re-create that merged attachment, hoping to regain the connection and to make up for its loss, and yet we have so much difficulty in achieving the second part of what is needed—boundaries and separated attachments. In childhood, we learned that we must transfer these needs for connection from mother to a man; now we replay that very same scenario. Just as we remember the taste of the satisfying, containing, fulfilling aspects of our attachment to mother, so too do we now remember the bonds with our women friends. What we really need, and perhaps what women find most impossible, is to have *both* satisfying couple relationships and meaningful attachments to women friends.

Ruth and Nellie began their friendship when they were both in their late twenties and both single. They spent nearly every weekend together and shared the ins and outs of their various and ever-changing love affairs with men. Ruth was the first to marry and, at that time, Nellie was seriously involved with Joe. The couples went out together and Ruth and Nellie continued to spend time on their own. Nellie and Joe began to live together and for the following two years the friendship continued on a smooth course. Then Ruth and her husband split up. During the time of the separation and divorce, Nellie was very involved and supportive. Ruth was a mess. She spent many evenings with Nellie and Joe, even sleeping at their apartment on the nights that she felt too upset to be on her own. She was worried that she was an imposition, but both Nellie and Joe kept assuring her that she wasn't. Gradually, she began to recover from the divorce and to feel her old self again. She fixed up her apartment, replacing things that Adam had taken to his new place. She still found it difficult and unusual to be on her own, but the acute pain was now a thing of the past.

Ruth and Nellie still arranged regular dates with one another, but now their availability to the friendship was no longer parallel. When they were both in couples, their need for each other matched perfectly. Now Ruth felt a gap between them. This was particularly acute on the weekend when Nellie was spending time with Joe. Ruth felt very much on her own. She knew that she could not expect Nellie to go out with her on Friday or Saturday evening because this was traditional couple time, but it was precisely at those times that she felt most acutely alone and in need of her friend. She felt very awkward going out to dinner or a movie on her own and had to push herself each and every time. She found herself waiting for Nellie to suggest a date because she didn't want always to be the one who seemed interested or needy. Because Ruth was not in a couple, her dependency on Nellie was more apparent. Although she knew that Nellie was dependent upon her as well, Nellie's dependency was somehow hidden within her couple relationship. Ruth was already feeling too vulnerable and exposing her need, even to her best friend, made her feel humiliated. At times it felt as though the whole world was in couples, her best friend was happy and loved, and that she would never again live a normal life.

Meanwhile, Nellie, too, had to adjust to the change in their lives. She knew that Ruth's situation was a very difficult one. She knew other women who were single or divorced and in their thirties who were feeling desperate about the possibility of ever meeting a suitable man. Nellie was aware of Ruth's need for a friend who could be much more available and felt inadequate at providing that kind of companionship. She loved Ruth and her own need for Ruth didn't diminish. She often felt guilty for having Joe to go home to and imagined the pain and loneliness that her best friend must be feeling. At times Nellie felt that she was pulling herself in two directions. Neither Joe nor Ruth actually did anything to contribute to that feeling. In fact, each seemed very sensitive to and aware of her attachment to the other. In therapy, Nellie discussed her feeling that she was always apologizing to one or the other of them. She suffered from a continual feeling that she was either neglecting Joe or Ruth. She found herself fighting with Joe more frequently, feeling that the relationship had deteriorated and that she might have to end it. She also felt increasingly annoyed with Ruth. One minute she didn't like Ruth's passiveness, the next she didn't like Ruth's demands. As these feelings were explored in the therapy, we came to see that Nellie was having difficulty in maintaining two close attachments, one with a woman and one with a man. Her anger with each of them was a distancing mechanism. She was not comfortable with that much love and security. She felt undeserving of this luxury. She felt guilty in relation to Ruth, knowing that she had something that Ruth wanted but didn't have. It seemed so emotionally unfamiliar to her to have each of them accepting her attachment to the other. *Her attachment with one signified her separateness from the other. Thus, her multiple attachments caused her anxiety.* The pulls she experienced were of an internal nature and were, in fact, pulls at her merged attachments. Her guilt and anger toward each of them represented her internal juggling act—distancing herself first from one and then the other in an effort to preserve the equilibrium of the merged attachments.

This difficulty in believing that one can have a loving attachment to both a man and a woman at the same time has historical roots. We've seen how women transfer the original merged attachment with mother to both their relationships with other women as well as to their relationships with men. And just as psychological separation and autonomy presented difficulties within the mother–daughter relationship, so too do we anticipate those very same restrictions within our couple relationships and friendships. In other words, as we experience our husbands or lovers as mother, we unconsciously feel the pull not to abandon them. Attachment elsewhere, which represents a step toward separateness, seems to threaten the original relationship. Also, because traditionally so few fathers shared in the nurturing and raising of children, it is rare for us to have had a secure and loving attachment to both mother and to father, and thus, having the love of a woman friend and the love of a male partner is unfamiliar territory. Having both kinds of loving relationships can feel like having *too* much.

Another, possibly simultaneous, dynamic ensues for many women whose mothers' marriages were obviously disappointing; having a fulfilling and satisfying relationship can feel like a betrayal of mother. It exposes what she did not have; it exposes her loneliness; it exposes her pain. Our unconscious loyalty to mother finds us sabotaging potentially good relationships for how can we leave her all alone? We must stay with her in the sadness, the deprivation, the emptiness. It is very difficult to have so much when mother had so little. It is difficult to feel that deserving, that entitled to so much love and security.

Ruth and Nellie were each grappling, from different positions, with these complex dynamics. A whole new dimension was added when Nellie became pregnant. She felt extremely anxious about telling Ruth. She knew that Ruth would be happy for her, but how could Ruth help but feel awful at the same time? She told Ruth about it over a lunch date and Ruth responded with genuine excitement and pleasure, asking appropriate questions about the due date, the obstetrical arrangements, and so on. Neither woman brought up what this might mean to their relationship, although each was privately wondering. When they parted, Nellie felt relieved that the news was out and appreciative of her friend's ability to be so emotionally generous. Ruth, on the other hand, was overwhelmed with thoughts and feelings. She was truly happy for Nellie and Joe. She loved them dearly and knew that the pregnancy was making them very happy. She felt frightened about the impending changes in Nellie's life and knew that once a baby was born, Nellie would be even less available to their friendship. She felt a deep sadness that she and Nellie could not share this experience together, as they had other milestones in their lives. She felt frightened at the thought that she might never be in a relationship in which she, too, could have a baby.

Throughout the pregnancy, things changed only slightly. Nellie talked with Ruth about the pregnancy, the birth plans, and her plans for part-time work. Ruth continued to talk with Nellie about her work, her occasional dates, and her despair about the dating scene. They were in two very different places in their lives, but their friendship was such that it could weather those differences. Then the baby was born. Although Ruth knew that things would be different, the extent of Nellie's involvement with the baby went far beyond what she had imagined. In the first months of Tessa's life, Nellie and Joe seemed totally absorbed. Every conversation, every interest was related to Tessa. Ruth loved Tessa and felt closer to her than she ever had to any baby, so to some extent the discussions about every detail of Tessa's development were of interest. But Ruth found herself having to make another significant adjustment in her relationship with Nellie. Nellie's attachment to Joe and now to an even more dependent Tessa meant that her availability to the friendship had decreased dramatically. Going out on their own became a rare treat. Ruth knew rationally that this was not to do with Nellie losing affection for her, for she could see that Nellie had very little time to herself, but it was painful and difficult nonetheless.

As several months went by, Nellie began to feel back to her old self again. She longed for some time alone with Ruth and other women friends and yet she found it very difficult to get that time. She already felt guilty for going back to work and being away from Tessa for so many hours, and so arranging social dates for herself was fraught with tension. She tried to talk on the telephone with Ruth several times a week and felt that Ruth was very understanding about the circumstances of her life. They both seemed to hold on to the notion that as Tessa got older, things would ease up and they would have more time together.

Nellie and Ruth's situation is currently being reproduced in the lives of thousands of women. These two women were able to hold on to their friendship through three significant life changes: marriages, a divorce, and the birth of a child. Many other women have not been as fortunate. In recent years, we have heard of many friendships that have not survived these kinds of changes. At times, the differences have created too great a gap, making identification, a central feature in women's friendships, impossible. Some women have found that they could not tackle the feelings of envy or competition that emerged as a result of a friend being in a couple, having a baby, or perhaps getting a divorce and getting out of an unsatisfactory relationship. To witness a friend having or doing what one would like for herself is too painful to stay in contact with. But surely the loss of a woman friend, the loss of that special and much-needed woman-to-woman contact, is just as painful.

Perhaps now, precisely because women are struggling to create and maintain their separate identities, it is for the first time possible for women to have both attachment to friends and lovers. Attachment that does not stem from a merged attachment, but rather from a genuine, separated attachment. The stresses and strains of managing work, partners, children, and friends are very real. At times, it feels as though there aren't enough days in the week to manage them all. But women are experimenting, adjusting, and juggling their time in order to have the things that feel necessary for a sense of well-being. Maybe women today cannot spend as much time as they once did or as they would like with their women friends. But in breaking free of our merged attachments, and, more importantly, by forging new *separated* attachments, we can hope to make up for the loss of quantity with a new quality of women's friendships; friendships just as rich, just as intimate, just as caring, but also more flexible, more open to difficulties and differences. We cannot afford to sacrifice the ones we need the most. In developing a new feminine identity, a separated identity, we must believe in our entitlement to the love of others, both women and men, so that the meaning of separateness will include attachment.

Chapter 10

Separated Attachments/ Connected Autonomy

Eight women psychotherapists, between the ages of thirty-four and fifty-eight, meet in New York to discuss their work and break down some of the isolation that comes with private practice. Two of the women have grown children, four of the women have young children, two women do not have children, though one is planning to get pregnant in the coming year. Three sessions in and the group is talking about stress. Stress related to work, to juggling work with raising young children, to earning enough money to pay for the apartment that must now be bought. Stress related to not having time for relaxation or fun. Stress related to not having enough leisure time to spend with husbands and partners. Stress related to the pressure to read technical material, to continue to learn when one feels one can barely find the time to pay the bills. Sighs of acknowledgment are heard throughout the room as a woman speaks. Giggles of recognition punctuate the sentences. The personal experience of losing a babysitter is heard one moment; in the next the women speak of capitalism and how feminism has been corrupted, taken over, taking us along with it. The personal and the political, all in one discussion. There is something thrillingly reminiscent of earlier times. And as the women talk about the stress in their lives, there is both the pain of the reality as well as a feeling of hope and optimism. Once again, here we are: women talking about things that do not feel right, being critical of the system that directs us to these points, questioning our choices, our options. As women together, we discuss the new wave of isolated feelings; guilt about not being with our children or partners enough; envy of the success of other women; competitive feelings that arise when making the decision about whether to read a journal article or relax and read a novel. There is relief in the telling. Joy as the other women nod their heads in understanding and agreement when what we feared was disgust and rejection. The stress that we were speaking about seemed to dissolve bit by bit. Women supporting women. Women being accepted and cared for by other women. Personal pain and self-hatred being translated into social critique.

There was also something noticeably different from a women's group of fifteen years ago. Each woman was professionally defined. Each woman earned an adequate income. Each woman had either already had children or had come to some resolution about getting pregnant or not having children. We were no longer talking about constraints of women's traditional position. We were no longer facing the enormous hurdles of creating ourselves in the world outside of the home. On the contrary, some of the women expressed longing at the mere thought of spending uninterrupted time with the children or puttering around the house. Things have changed.

Although this is a particular group of women representative of a particular professional, class, and ethnic makeup, in many ways the issues these women spoke of concern a multitude of women today. Whether or not one was an active agent in changing the social position of women, one cannot escape the impact of these changes. As with other significant social movements and reforms (civil rights, for example), at one moment the results seem to have been incorporated so gradually as to be barely noticeable, while at another one sees that truly dramatic social changes have occurred in a virtual blink of the eye. We live in a new era. The era of women working outside the home as well as in the family; the era of rising divorce rates; the era of an increase in single women and women without children; the era of child care; the era of shifting domestic and economic responsibilities.

The women in this new women's group were fortunate enough to sit down together to talk about their concerns. In admitting to the feelings that each previously held inside herself, came hope, optimism, and energy, somewhat counteracting isolation, depression, self-hatred, guilt, anger. Another noticeable and monumental difference in this 1980s women's group was the number of times a woman said, "Yes, I know what you mean, but I don't experience it in the same way. For me . . ." One was able to listen to another's feelings and predicament, to feel empathy, to offer support *and yet not have to be either the same as or silent about the differences in order to preserve the feelings of safety.* For the most part, each could tolerate and acknowledge that there were eight individuated women in the room and still feel the support and the care from another woman. This most important occurrence reflects the historical progression in women's psychology. For in this new consciousness-raising group, the women were able to be separate, individuated people who were also empathic, care giving, loving, and connected. *The differentiation did not dissolve the connection. This psychological achievement and its significance as a social and psychological development is a key to the resolution of the current problems in women's relationships.*

Throughout this book, we have seen women who are struggling with the critical issues of separateness and connection in relationships with other women. Over and over again, we have seen how one seems to threaten the other, how difficult it is for a woman to feel that she can get support and love from another woman without offering her very self in exchange. We have seen the ways in which our psychologies, developed and shaped in very particular ways within our culture, have us colluding in the repression of our*selves*.

And yet, within every form of oppression lies the seeds of liberation. Although women have suffered because historically work has been divided according to gender, this division of labor has nevertheless produced vital sensibilities in women. The responsibility of raising infants and children demands attention, care, concern, and awareness for the well-being of another. The mother-child relationship sensitizes women to the needs of others. As the managers of the domestic, personal, and emotional spheres, women have retained an ability for human connection. Our traditional restricted social roles are enabling because they develop our capacity to connect and nurture, but they are also disabling because they restrain our autonomy and separateness. In the same dialectical fashion, the patriarchal context of the world women are now emerging into—the masculine world of competition and the repression of emotions—has its liberating aspects, because they encourage, even demand self-development that will ultimately produce a new synthesis, a new femininity that is connected and caring as well as separate and defined.

In the 1980s we are witnessing the tension between a traditional mode that seeks to incorporate some women into the existing structure, and far-reaching change that reveals the need for more social and psychological equality between women and men in the world inside and outside the home. Tradition aims to put the brakes on the gains of the 1960s for women and blacks, and by granting equality to a token number of each, declares we have been successful and need demand no more. But what has really changed if one accepts that vision? Is it that we are now allowed the honor of being more like men? Do we want that?

We think not. Men, too, have suffered as a result of this competitive, alienated form of social relations. Men have been severely emotionally constrained and disabled by the mandates by which they have had to live. Far from needing women to be more like men, we need men to be more like women. That is, not only do women need to have more freedom to develop their creative potential outside of the domestic sphere, but men need to develop themselves *within* the domestic sphere. In chapter 2, we discussed some of the effects of women entering the "male" milieu. And throughout this book we've seen the damaging psychological effects of the social restrictions women and men have suffered. The social and the psychological go hand in hand; changes in one produce a ripple effect in the other. In many ways, we have all moved along on the wave of history. We've made choices, but those choices are themselves produced by the social climate of the time. What seems like an appropriate choice at one point may be, and yet further down the road we reflect and see that perhaps the choice has led us on a path we don't want to be on. And so we make another choice and keep moving. More and more women and men seem aware that following the traditional path for men is not the road to personal satisfaction. Stress, high blood pressure, heart attacks at an early age, drinking problems, alienation from one's children and partner need not be reproduced. Striving for autonomy, for psychological well-being and separateness, while maintaining a balance of connectedness in our relationships with partners, friends, and children seems more appropriately to promise to meet the needs of women, men, and children.

Creating the balance between autonomy and connectedness is becoming ever more critical, both socially and psychologically. It has been our intention to demonstrate that it is within women's friendships that the historical conflict of these two forces is apparent. The feelings of competition, envy, abandonment, and betrayal are symptoms of this conflict. We've seen that within each of these feelings there is an expression of the wanting, the longing, the desire for self-actualization, the rage at restrictions and oppression. The current expression of these feelings is personal and isolated and pushes each woman who feels them into further retreat.

These feelings divide women and distance them from one another, leaving them to feel mistrust and fear.

It is now, perhaps more than ever, that the social and psychological pieces overlap such that women need something quite specific from each other. We have shown the ways in which the 1970s reproduced in many ways aspects of the earliest years in the mother-daughter relationship. That is the acknowledgment of the need for other women, and the respect and love each woman received as she gave it to others sowed the seeds for further self-development. And yet just at the point where we had perhaps gotten a taste of self-love, the first step toward separation-individuation, we stopped short. First, the forces and the power of patriarchy reached out to us and allowed some of us under its wing. Second, we stumbled on the steps of differentiation and separation. Having never had the experience of successful and permissible separation and differentiation, we could not adequately provide it to one another.

Today, women have the possibility of allowing each other differences; of supporting the choices to become mothers or not to become mothers; of recognizing the differences in the lives of single women and women in couples. We have the opportunity to acknowledge our need for other women and our need for recognition and acceptance of our autonomous selves. This time around, we can provide this to each other.

Two women, separate yet connected: each woman feels whole within herself. Each woman feels her continuing need for intimate relationships with both a woman (women) and a man (men). Each woman is able to see the other for who she is, in a distinct and differentiated way. Each woman feels that she is seen in this way by her friend. Each woman feels secure in her attachment to her friend. Each woman acknowledges the interdependency between them. It is within this kind of woman-to-woman relationship that giving is possible; a giving not based on need and identification, nor on a need to connect in order to exist, nor on a search for oneself in the attachment, nor on a merged attachment. But rather a giving that draws on women's ability to listen, to empathize, to feel, to extend a hand, to care.

Some women fear that if they were able to care for themselves, if they were all right, if they no longer operated out of merged attachments, they would not need anyone. They would no longer want to give to anyone else. They would be alone. In fact, this is never the case. For the more internal security one has, the easier it becomes to be more vulnerable and more emotionally open. One's expression of need becomes an acceptable aspect of emotional life rather than a dreaded exposure of an insecure or inevitably lacking self. With a clear boundary between self and other, the more the resources one has for both giving and receiving.

Moving from merged attachments to separated attachments is an enormous task, and yet we are halfway there. We know that the feelings express not only the desire for separation and autonomy, but the desires for connection, for nurturance, for intimacy as well. And as we have seen for all of the women we have described, the ability or the desire to connect with other women is present. The familiarity, the identifications, the tools of emotional responsiveness and care giving resonate for every woman in her relationships with other women. Women provide other women with feelings of safety, excitement, calm, warmth, intellectual stimulation, joie de vivre. Whether it be women friends sitting in the park watching the children together, starting a business together, shopping together, sharing a lunch break together, or collaborating on a book together, the camaraderie and connection fulfill a basic human need. In striving for separated attachments, we are not beginning at square one. We have a strong foundation upon which to build, for women know how to connect, know how to give care and attention, know how to be aware of the needs of others. We must believe in those connections enough, trust them enough, rely on them enough, acknowledge them enough, to let go of the merged attachment. Only this time around we will let go from a position of plenty, of love for ourselves and therefore other women, of knowing we can still have more, of knowing that letting go is giving birth.

Notes

1. Now incorporated into the College of Staten Island, The City University of New York.

2. *See* Luise Eichenbaum and Susie Orbach, *Understanding Women: A Feminist Psychoanalytic Approach* (New York: Basic Books, 1983).

3. The New York Feminist Therapists Study Group, 1973–75.

4. The center has not attracted many black or Asian women. This is most likely because there have been no black or Asian therapists on staff who might provide an easier bridge for those seeking therapy.

5. Over the last five years we've been joined by Susan Gutwill, Anne Leiner, Andrea Gitter, Lela Zaphiropoulos, and Laurie Phillips.

6. Of course, this is far from the truth. Women's economic position is not improving, and although new vistas have opened up, equality at work and home is a long way off.

7. Jean Baker Miller, in trying to rescue women's experience from the pathologizing of a patriarchal psychiatric establishment, has argued that since women's identity is formed within

the nexus of relationships, male concepts of separation-in-dividuation are not useful in describing the psychological development of women. Such concepts are superimposed upon a situation which they patently don't fit. In this, Jean Baker Miller is undoubtedly right, for women experience their sense of identity in relationship. They know themselves in the context of the ebb and flow between themselves and others. But the problems with drawing one's self-identity in this way has negative as well as positive consequences. In trying to understand the sources of some of the difficulties in women's relationships with each other, an understanding of the underbelly of these connections is essential. "The Development of Women's Sense of Self" from the *Work in Progress Series of the Stone Center for Developmental Services and Studies,* 1984.

8. In her book, *Feminine Leadership or How to Succeed in Business Without Being One of the Boys* (New York: Times Books, 1985), Marilyn Loden makes a strong case for the potential of creating new forms of feminine leadership that do not replicate the traditional masculine competitive ones. She points out that throughout the 1970s in business there was a tremendous lack of worker interest and commitment. Psychologists called in as consultants to develop ways to cope with these problems proposed a change to a more personal mode. Loden argues that the more personal mode is a trend that complements feminization of the work place and that women's skills have more of a place in these newly developing mores. Not only will there be less of a split between what is feminine and what constitutes leadership, but women will be seen to have the essential skills which all successful managers must learn, thereby giving women their rightful recognition and respect. The current mandate that a woman adapt herself to fit in to a male mode may not be the only option.

9. Lillian Rubin, *Just Friends: The Role of Friendship in Our Lives* (New York: Harper & Row, 1985), pp. 83 and 89.

10. *See* Luise Eichenbaum and Susie Orbach, *What Do Women Want: Exploding the Myth of Dependency* (New York: Coward

McCann, 1983), for discussion of the developmental differences that lead to men's difficulties with connection and intimacy and women's difficulties with separation and intimacy.

11. *See* Eichenbaum and Orbach, *Understanding Women.*

12. *See* Susie Orbach, *Fat Is a Feminist Issue* (New York: Paddington Press, 1978); also, *Hunger Strike: The Anorectic's Struggle as a Metaphor for Our Age* (New York: Norton, 1986.)

13. Over the last decade, Harriet Goldhor Lerner in *The Dance of Anger* (New York: Harper & Row, 1985) and Teresa Bernades-Bonesatti in "Women and Anger: Conflicts with Aggression in Contemporary Women," *Journal of the American Medical Women's Association* 33 (1978), pp. 215–19, have made some extremely interesting and useful contributions to an understanding of women's anger, placing women's difficulties with expressing and feeling anger within a psychosocial context.

14. *See* Eichenbaum and Orbach, *What Do Women Want.*

15. Robert J. Stoller, *Sex and Gender: On the Development of Masculinity and Femininity* (New York: Science House, 1968); and Eichenbaum and Orbach, *What Do Women Want.*

16. *See* Stoller, *Sex and Gender;* and Eichenbaum and Orbach, *What Do Women Want.*

Selected Bibliography

Belotti, E. G. *Little Girls.* London: Writers & Readers, 1977.

Block, J. D., and D. Greenberg. *Women & Friendship.* New York: Franklin Watts, 1985.

Chodorow, N. *The Reproduction of Mothering, Psychoanalysis and the Sociology of Gender.* Berkley: University of California Press, 1978.

Dinnerstein, D. *The Mermaid and the Minotaur.* New York: Harper & Row, 1976.

Eichenbaum, L., and S. Orbach. *Understanding Women: A Feminist Psychoanalytic Approach.* New York: Basic Books, 1983.

Faderman, Lilian. *Surpassing the Love of Men.* London: The Women's Press, 1985.

Fairbairn, W. R. D. *Psychoanalytic Studies of the Personality.* London: Routledge, Kegan Paul, 1952.

Friday, N. *Jealousy.* New York: William Morrow and Co., 1985.

Guntrip, H. *Schizoid Phenomena and Object Relations Theory.* New York: International Universities Press, 1969.

Klein, M. *Envy and Gratitude.* New York: Basic Books, 1975.

Lerner, H. *The Dance of Anger.* New York: Harper & Row, 1985.

Mahler, M., F. Pine, and A. Bergman. *The Psychological Birth of the Human Infant.* New York: Basic Books, 1975.

Margolies, E. *The Best of Friends, the Worst of Enemies.* New York: The Dial Press, 1975.

Money, J., and A. Erhardt. *Man and Woman, Boy and Girl: The Differentiation and Dimorphism of Gender Identity from Conception to Maturity.* Baltimore, Md.: John Hopkins Press, 1973.

Orbach, S. *Hunger Strike: The Anorectic's Struggle as a Metaphor for Our Age.* New York: Norton, 1986.

Raymond, J. A. *Passion for Friends.* Boston: Beacon Press, 1986.

Rich, A. *On Lies, Secrets, and Silence.* New York: Norton, 1979.

Rubin, L. *Just Friends: The Role of Friendship in Our Lives.* New York: Harper & Row, 1985.

Spitz, R. *The First Year of Life: A Psychoanalytic Study of Normal and Deviant Development of Object Relations.* New York: International Universities Press, 1965.

Winnicott, D. W. *The Maturational Processes and the Facilitating Environment.* New York: International Universities Press, 1965.

———. *Primary Maternal Preoccupation: Through Pediatrics to Psycho-Analysis.* New York: Basic Books, 1958.

Index